WND Books
COLLECTOR'S EDITION

All the best

RAY COMFORT

WHAT HOLLYWOOD BELIEVES

AN INTIMATE LOOK AT THE FAITH OF THE FAMOUS

THE PERSONAL BELIEFS OF:

Bruce Willis, Kevin Costner,

Britney Spears, Michael J. Fox,

Rod Steiger, Arnold Schwarzenegger,

George Lucas, Jack Nicholson,

Madonna, Michael Jackson,

Hugh Hefner, John Wayne,

Goldie Hawn, Robert Duvall,

Rosie O'Donnell, Jim Carrey...

genesis
PUBLISHING GROUP

What Hollywood Believes:
An Intimate Look at the Faith of the Famous

Published by
Genesis Publishing Group
2002 Skyline Place
Bartlesville, OK 74006
www.genesis-group.net

Edited by Lynn Copeland

Cover, page design, and production by Genesis Group

Printed in the United States of America

ISBN 0-9749300-1-6

Unless otherwise indicated, Scripture quotations are from the *New King James Version*, © 1979, 1980, 1982 by Thomas Nelson Inc., Publishers, Nashville, Tennessee.

Scripture references marked KJV are from the *King James Version*.

Scripture quotations designated Amplified are from *The Amplified Bible*, © 1965 by Zondervan Publishing House, Grand Rapids, Michigan.

For more information, visit **www.whatHollywoodbelieves.com**.

To
DARREL & TAMMY
RUNDUS

CONTENTS

HOLLYWOOD AND GOD 9

Aames, Willie 101
Affleck, Ben 47
Allen, Woody .109
Alley, Kirstie 43
Amos, Tori .86
Anderson, Pamela 99
Aykroyd, Dan .74
Baldwin, Alec .72
Basinger, Kim 67
Berry, Halle .30
Bono 21
Boone, Pat 147
Brando, Marlon 75
Caine, Michael 83
Cameron-Bure, Candace 86
Cameron, Kirk 150
Carrey, Jim .23
Cash, Johnny 122
Cassidy, Shaun 35
Cavett, Dick .68
Caviezel, Jim 127
Chaplin, Charlie 57
Clooney, George 93
Cole, Natalie 130
Collins, Judy .18

Cooper, Alice 143
Costner, Kevin 142
Couric, Katie 65
Cruise, Tom 127
Cyrus, Billy Ray 26
Diller, Phyllis 97
Dillon, Matt 123
Disney, Walt 59
Douglas, Kirk 39
Duvall, Robert 50
Dylan, Bob 19
Eden, Barbara 108
Evans, Linda 78
Fishburne, Laurence 41
Fisher, Carrie 104
Flynt, Larry 110
Foster, Jodie 114
Fox, Michael J. 144
Franken, Al 44
Gates, Bill 124
Gere, Richard 137
Gibson, Mel 38
Gifford, Kathie Lee 149
Glover, Danny 67
Griffith, Andy 147
Hawn, Goldie 142
Hayes, Isaac 117
Heaton, Patricia .138
Hefner, Hugh 24
Hepburn, Katharine 73
Heston, Charlton .31
Houston, Whitney 117
Ireland, Kathy 93
Jackson, Janet 62
Jackson, LaToya 81

Jackson, Michael 27
Jackson, Victoria 131
Jennings, Peter 42
Jesus of Nazareth 157
Joel, Billy 81
Jones, Dean .151
Joyner-Kersee, Jackie 111
King, Stephen 22
Lennon, John 57
Lewis, Jerry .103
Lucas, George 13
MacLaine, Shirley 60
Madonna 63
Maher, Bill .132
Mandrell, Barbara 130
Manson, Marilyn 118
McGraw, Dr. Phil 100
McLeod, Gavin 140
Miller, Dennis 51
Minnelli, Liza 112
Mr. T 125
Moore, Michael 101
Nicholson, Jack 28
Nimoy, Leonard 33
Nolte, Nick .48
Norris, Chuck 69
O'Hara, Maureen 99
O'Donnell, Rosie 141
Parton, Dolly 14
Peck, Gregory 49
Pitt, Brad 54
Reagan, Ronald 129
Reese, Della .96
Reeve, Christopher 113
Reynolds, Debbie 36

Rooney, Andy 105
Rooney, Mickey 126
Russell, Jane 41
Ryder, Winona 148
Schwarzenegger, Arnold 16
Shatner, William 80
Sheen, Martin 139
Shriver, Maria .32
Simon, Neil 102
Sinatra, Frank .82
Spears, Britney 151
Steiger, Rod 20
Stern, Howard .20
Stewart, Jimmy 53
Taylor, Elizabeth 112
Taylor, James .18
Teller (of Penn & Teller) 72
Tesh, John 40
Tomlin, Lily 149
Travolta, John .14
Urich, Robert 120
Washington, Denzel 120
Wayne, John 66
Welles, Orson .70
Whelchel, Lisa .34
Wilder, Gene 71
Willis, Bruce 87
Winfrey, Oprah 121
Young, Loretta 52

CONCLUSION 173

SAVE YOURSELF SOME PAIN 175

PSALM 51 193

NOTES 195

HOLLYWOOD
AND GOD

Despite what the press may convey, America is *not* antagonistic toward the things of God. According to a March 2004 Associated Press poll, an incredible 87 percent of respondents wanted "under God" kept in the Pledge of Allegiance.[1] Contrary to expectations, the blockbuster movie *The Passion of the Christ* grossed hundreds of millions of dollars in its opening weeks, proving that Americans have a strong interest in God. A Gallup poll shortly after the film's release found that three in four Americans have seen it or expect to see it.[2]

The New York Times reported, "As the overwhelming success of *The Passion of the Christ* reverberates through Hollywood, producers and studio executives are asking whether the movie industry has been neglecting large segments of the American audience eager for more openly religious fare."[3]

What Hollywood Believes explores an area that *has* been neglected in the past—the religious faith of the famous. It is a sad irony that when legendary filmmaker Cecil B. DeMille (director of the epic movie *The Ten Commandments*) first came to California in the early 1900s, he settled in a small town that was giving away free land to anyone willing to build a place of worship. The town, said to be a "Christian" settlement, had a picturesque name—Hollywood.[4]

Yet through the years the famous town has come to bear little resemblance to middle America. For example, a survey conducted among the 104 top television writers and executives found only 49 percent consider adultery to be wrong—which means 51 percent believe adultery is morally right. Meanwhile 85 percent of the rest of America believes adultery is wrong.[5]

When asked about their religious affiliations, 45 percent of Hollywood executives said they had none, while the general population citing no religious affiliation was a mere 4 percent. Gallup polls reveal that over 90 percent of Americans believe in God, with as many as 40 percent attending worship services regularly,[6] yet America's true religious nature hasn't been reflected in television shows or movies.

While I had a wonderful time researching for this book, discovering the stars' beliefs was arduous and time-consuming. Because Hollywood has for many years been under the illusion that America isn't interested in God, many celebrities hide their spiritual beliefs for fear of jeopardizing their careers. (Some of the quotes are therefore very short, for which I apologize.[7]) Each time I uncovered something a famous person believed about spirituality, it was like finding a golden needle in a huge haystack of information.

So what you are about to read is unique. The spiritual beliefs of the famous have not often been published—especially in a single resource such as this book. The utmost care has been taken to cite all sources of information, in the belief that each of the sources is accurate.

These findings are both fascinating and informative. Not surprisingly, celebrities expressed a wide range of views. One star thinks God is a woman, while others believe they will be reincarnated. Some beliefs are a little off the wall; others seem to make sense... but who am I to say who is right and who is wrong?

However, if I were researching the thoughts of famous football players on how the game should be played, and found conflicting beliefs on how the players should line up for the snap, it would be sensible for me to go to a respected source of information—the *standard* for football plays. I would use that as a plumb line to compare how far to the left or right each player stood.

That's what I have done with this book. In it you will find extremes. So I have gone to the most respected source for spirituality, not only for Jews and Christians but also for many other major religions. I have compared the beliefs of the famous to the bestselling Book of all time, the Book that has stood the *test* of time—the Bible. This is because I don't want *What Hollywood Believes* to be merely informational. I want it also to be *educational*—so that each of us can think beyond what the celebrities say and perhaps even beyond our own beliefs. And the best way to do this is to consider these beliefs in view of a plumb line.

We'll be in good company as we do so. Many of our country's great leaders have looked to the Bible as an educational tool as well as a source of wisdom.

Theodore Roosevelt firmly believed, "A thorough knowledge of the Bible is worth more than a college education."[8] Dwight D. Eisenhower stated, "The Bible is endorsed by the ages. Our civilization is built upon its words. In no other Book is there such a collection of inspired wisdom, reality, and hope."[9] John Quincy Adams had similar convictions: "The first and almost the only Book deserving of universal attention is the Bible...It is an invaluable and inexhaustible mine of knowledge and virtue."[10] His father, John Adams, said simply, "The Bible is the best Book in the world."[11]

Commendations for the Bible aren't limited to presidents. The "Father of Science," Sir Isaac Newton, asserted, "We account the Scriptures of God to be the most sublime philosophy. I find more sure marks of authenticity in the Bible than in any profane history whatsoever."[12]

With these thoughts in mind, I hope you will find this publication more than titillating. I trust it will help you to see that many of those celebrities to whom we look up are also looking up...toward the heavens. Although they are rich, famous, successful, and seemingly self-sufficient, they have the same fears, doubts, and aspirations as the rest of us.

In these pages I have also attempted to address some of the difficulties and objections raised by celebrities as well as others—such as the issue of suffering, proof that God exists, why we should believe a Book that is full of strange stories, who made God, etc.

Researching the content for this book has caused me to not only be more educated about other people's beliefs, but it has helped me to grow in my own faith. I hope it does the same for you. So let's now look at the faith of the famous, and see what they believe.

BIRTH NAME: George Walton Lucas, Jr.
DATE OF BIRTH: May 14, 1944
PLACE OF BIRTH: Modesto, California
OCCUPATIONS: Director, Writer, Producer
CLAIM TO FAME: *Star Wars* (1977)—earned 11 Oscar nominations

GEORGE LUCAS

I n discussing the religious overtones of *Star Wars*, George Lucas explained, "I put the Force into the movie in order to try to awaken a certain kind of spirituality in young people—more a belief in God than a belief in any particular religious system. I wanted to make it so that young people would begin to ask questions about the mystery. Not having enough interest in the mysteries of life to ask the question, 'Is there a God or is there not a God?' —that is for me the worst thing that can happen. I think you should have an opinion about that. Or you should be saying, 'I'm looking. I'm very curious about this, and I am going to continue to look until I can find an answer, and if I can't find an answer, then I'll die trying.' I think it's important to have a belief system and to have faith."[13]

When his interviewer asked, "Do you have an opinion, or are you looking?" Lucas replied, "I think there is a God. No question. What that God is or what we know about that God, I'm not sure."[14]

George Lucas said that he had "more a belief in God than a belief in any particular religious system." This is a phrase that you will see is often repeated in this book by celebrities. They have the good sense to separate "God" from the cold religious system that so often portrays itself as the divine representative.

BIRTH NAME: Dolly Rebecca Parton
DATE OF BIRTH: January 19, 1946
PLACE OF BIRTH: Locust Ridge, Tennessee
OCCUPATIONS: Actress, Writer, Musician, Producer, Composer
CLAIM TO FAME: Hit single "Here You Come Again" (1977)

DOLLY PARTON

Dolly Parton recalled, "My grandpa was a preacher, and I guess at an impressionable age, I believed that through God I could do everything. And I still have a lot of faith in God, as I perceive Him, and that's why so many of my songs have an inspirational feeling.

"Everybody thinks of God as a different thing. To me, God is that greater, higher energy—that greater, wiser wisdom. It's that thing in all of us that we all have to draw from. I've always trusted God and trusted myself, which to me are intertwined. I'm a creative person, and what gifts I have come from that divine place that I try to tap into. So who have I got to be afraid of?"[15]

BIRTH NAME: John Joseph Travolta
DATE OF BIRTH: February 18, 1954
PLACE OF BIRTH: Englewood, New Jersey
OCCUPATIONS: Actor, Musician
CLAIM TO FAME: Vinnie Barbarino on "Welcome Back, Kotter" (1975–1979)

JOHN TRAVOLTA

In speaking of his beliefs, John Travolta said, "When I was 21 years old, I found Scientology and that gave me a kind of sanity. The technology I found so brilliant, that that kind of put things in perspective for me. A film not doing well isn't a disaster—a plane crash is a disaster, you know what I mean?"[16]

As far as what happens after death, Travolta explained, "I think that the body ends and you as a spirit go on. It's up to you what you are going to do. It could be [reincarnation] if that is what you chose to do. You want to get back into another body or if you just want to hang out, whatever you feel like."[17]

When asked whether he believes in God, Travolta answered, "I think the whole idea of Scientology is to think for yourself... If you ask me personally, I think yes there's God. But each day through a lot of the studying that I do, I think I get to understand, possibly, what God is about but I don't think I fully get the picture yet."[18]

After stating that he prays, though not regularly, Travolta was asked, "Who or what would you be praying to?" He replied, "To the yet-not-fully-understood God concept."[19]

John Travolta, like the rest of us, doesn't fully get the picture yet. Who of us can say we completely understand God or even the mysteries of this life? The Bible says that "we see in a mirror dimly." There are many questions to which we haven't yet found adequate answers.

Despite this, surveys reveal that most people pray, even skeptics. A good dose of severe turbulence at 30,000 feet is enough to make any atheist backslide momentarily and request help from some Higher Being—even if it's just a one-word prayer uttered deep within the mind. The issue isn't whether we pray, but whether God answers our prayers.

God *does* answer prayer, but often not in a way most of us would want or even expect. Undoubtedly, most of our prayers are selfish, such as for health and wealth. For reasons only He knows, God sometimes says yes and sometimes says no. And sometimes He says, "Wait for a while."

BIRTH NAME: Arnold Alois Schwarzenegger
DATE OF BIRTH: July 30, 1947
PLACE OF BIRTH: Thal, Styria, Austria
OCCUPATIONS: Bodybuilder, Actor, California Governor
CLAIM TO FAME: Five-time Mr. Universe titleholder,
The Terminator (1984)

ARNOLD SCHWARZENEGGER

When asked about his belief in God, Arnold Schwarzenegger said, "I believe in God and I believe, therefore, in the opposite: the devil and evil forces. Everyone has their own interpretation of that. Some people think the devil—they take the 'd' away and you have evil. Is there something up in the clouds? Probably not. But we, as people, are much better off if we do believe in good and evil."[20]

Although his mother took him to church every Sunday, he rebelled at age 18 or 19. Schwarzenegger recalls, "I thought the whole thing was absolutely absurd. When you get older, and especially when you have children, ... all of a sudden you start thinking back to what your parents taught you and what you rebelled against. And suddenly it makes sense and you teach it to your kids. In a couple of years they will rebel. It's the same cycle."[21]

It's not uncommon for people to cast off their religious beliefs when they encounter something they find "absurd" or that they don't understand. Let's take a logical look at this way of thinking.

Let's say that you are sitting on a plane. I convince you that you have to jump at any moment. You see your danger and put on a parachute. At that point you are saved from the jump. Your problem is totally dealt with. You have the parachute on, and that's all you need.

I then hand you the emergency card from the seat pocket so that you can become further informed about the plane. You study it. It shows you the exits and explains the oxygen masks. It shows the location of the parachute, and how to put it on. It even points out a red whistle and the locality of the bright green ripcord.

Everything on the card matches what you know is on the plane, right down to the red whistle. This convinces you that the card you are holding is the right card for this plane, and that it was put there by the plane owners.

Let's say you see something on the card that doesn't make sense. It says the carpet is red, when it's actually blue. Are you going to rip the parachute off? Of course not! That would be a stupid thing to do. The fact that you don't understand *everything* on the card has no bearing on the fact that you're going to have to jump out of the airplane. The important issue is that you are wearing the parachute. The apparent discrepancy is inconsequential.

Now think of someone on the plane who is not wearing a parachute. He studies the emergency card and reads that the carpet is a different color than what's on his plane, so he concludes that the card isn't valid. Because of this seeming inconsistency he makes a decision to reject the offer of a parachute. Think of his plight. He is in terrible danger. He could have to jump at any time. If you try to convince him that the color of the carpet doesn't matter, you are wasting precious time. Besides, you have *a better way* to persuade him.

You simply show him the 25,000-foot jump. You talk about the law of gravity and what it will do to his frail body if he hits the ground at 120 mph. You make him sweat a little. When he looks at you with fear in his eyes, you tell him about the parachute. Once he has it on, you can discuss the color of the carpet to your heart's content. The important thing is that he is wearing the parachute. This is another principle we will look at further in this publication.

BIRTH NAME: Judy Collins
DATE OF BIRTH: May 1, 1939
PLACE OF BIRTH: Seattle, Washington
OCCUPATIONS: Singer, Actor, Composer
CLAIM TO FAME: Popular singer/songwriter of the '60s

JUDY COLLINS

Judy Collins spoke about how her faith helped her after a tragic suicide in her family. She said, "I was certainly raised in the Christian belief, but I have a practice that believes in all saints and all gurus. Anybody who's been on the journey can help me. I'm a multi-disciplinary person. I do a meditation discipline, which is probably eastern in its origins, but I think that everything helps."[22]

Asked whether she believes in heaven, Judy answered, "I think everybody has a different definition of heaven. I don't think I'm going to be greeted by vestal virgins, and I doubt if I'll be walking among the clouds with Voltaire. I might! We don't know...I believe in a spiritual existence. My beliefs would more closely parallel the idea of reincarnation, of the spirit not being destroyed but going on in some form or another."[23]

BIRTH NAME: James Vernon Taylor
DATE OF BIRTH: March 12, 1948
PLACE OF BIRTH: Boston, Massachusetts
OCCUPATIONS: Singer, Songwriter
CLAIM TO FAME: Hit album *Sweet Baby James* (1970)

JAMES TAYLOR

One of James Taylor's records had a theme of disbelief—trying to make sense of life without believing in God. He explained, "Well, I find myself with a strong spiritual need

—in the past five years, particularly. And, certainly, it's acknowledged as an important part of recovery from addiction. Yet, it's hard for me to find an actual handle for it. I'm not saying that it's not helpful to think of having a real handle on the universe, your own personal point of attachment. But...I think it's crazy. But it's an insanity that keeps us sane. You might call a lot of these songs 'spirituals for agnostics.'"[24]

He was asked, "Does not having faith in a personal God make it harder to stick with a 12-step recovery program?" James replied, "Twelve-step programs say an interesting thing: Either you have a God, or you are God and you don't want the job."[25]

BIRTH NAME: Robert Allen Zimmerman
DATE OF BIRTH: May 24, 1941
PLACE OF BIRTH: Duluth, Minnesota
OCCUPATIONS: Musician, Singer, Songwriter, Actor
CLAIM TO FAME: Leader of the "Beat Generation"

BOB DYLAN

Many years ago when Bob Dylan was questioned about his belief in God, he said, "I feel a heartfelt God. I don't particularly think that God wants me thinking about Him all the time. I think that would be a tremendous burden on Him, you know. He's got enough people asking Him for favors. He's got enough people asking Him to pull strings."[26]

When asked if he thought religion was repressive, Dylan said, "Well, religion is repressive to a certain degree. Religion is another form of bondage which man invents to get himself to God. But that's why Christ came. Christ didn't preach religion. He preached the Truth, the Way and the Life. He said He'd come to give life and life more abundantly. He talked about life, not necessarily religion...

"A religion which says you have to do certain things to get to God..., which is a religion which is by works: you can enter into the Kingdom by what you do, what you wear, what you say, how many times a day you pray, how many good deeds you may do... That type of religion will not get you into the Kingdom, that's true. However there is a Master Creator, a Supreme Being in the Universe."[27]

BIRTH NAME: Rod Steiger
DATE OF BIRTH: April 14, 1925
PLACE OF BIRTH: Westhampton, New York
OCCUPATION: Actor
CLAIM TO FAME: *In the Heat of the Night* (1967)

ROD STEIGER

Rod Steiger said, "That's all religion is—some principle you believe in...man has accomplished far more miracles than the God he invented. What a tragedy it is to invent a God and then suffer to keep him King."[28]

BIRTH NAME: Howard Allen Stern
DATE OF BIRTH: January 12, 1954
PLACE OF BIRTH: Queens, New York
OCCUPATIONS: Actor, Writer, TV/Radio Host
CLAIM TO FAME: Shock-jock host of his own radio show

HOWARD STERN

Howard Stern was asked, "How do you feel about religion and politics?" He responded, "I'm sickened by all religions. Religion has divided people. I don't think there's any difference between the pope wearing a large hat and parading around with a smoking purse and an African painting his face white and praying to a rock."[29]

BIRTH NAME: Paul David Hewson
DATE OF BIRTH: May 10, 1960
PLACE OF BIRTH: Dublin, Ireland
OCCUPATIONS: Musician, Lead Singer/Songwriter of U2
CLAIM TO FAME: Nominated for Nobel Peace Prize (1993)

BONO

Bono said, "I often wonder if religion is the enemy of God. It's almost like religion is what happens when the Spirit has left the building. God's Spirit moves through us and the world at a pace that can never be constricted by any one religious paradigm. I love that. You know, it says somewhere in the Scriptures that the Spirit moves like a wind—no one knows where it's come from or where it's going..."[30]

It is obvious that Bono has some sort of knowledge of God and the Bible in his background. "Somewhere in the Scriptures" is a reference to John chapter 3:

> There was a man of the Pharisees named Nicodemus, a ruler of the Jews. This man came to Jesus by night and said to Him, "Rabbi, we know that You are a teacher come from God; for no one can do these signs that You do unless God is with him."
>
> Jesus answered and said to him, "Most assuredly, I say to you, unless one is born again, he cannot see the kingdom of God." Nicodemus said to Him, "How can a man be born when he is old? Can he enter a second time into his mother's womb and be born?"

Jesus answered, "Most assuredly, I say to you, unless one is born of water and the Spirit, he cannot enter the kingdom of God. That which is born of the flesh is flesh, and that which is born of the Spirit is spirit. Do not marvel that I said to you, 'You must be born again.' The wind blows where it wishes, and you hear the sound of it, but cannot tell where it comes from and where it goes. So is everyone who is born of the Spirit." (verses 1–9)

Some people are of the opinion that U2 is a *Christian* rock band. But when questioned on the subject, Bono explained, "We really f—— up our corner of the Christian market...I love hymns and gospel music, but the idea of turning your music into a tool for evangelism is missing the point...The most powerful idea that's entered the world in the last few thousand years—the idea of grace —is the reason I would like to be a Christian."[31]

BIRTH NAME: Stephen Edwin King
DATE OF BIRTH: September 21, 1947
PLACE OF BIRTH: Portland, Maine
OCCUPATIONS: Writer, Actor, Director, Producer
CLAIM TO FAME: Horror novelist and screenwriter

STEPHEN KING

Stephen King was questioned by an interviewer, "I am curious to know why you've placed the existence of God into the foreground of your recent work?"

He replied, "I think he's always been there...God is different in different books because it depends on the people you're writing about. I don't see myself as God's stenographer. As someone who believes in God, believes that God is a logical outgrowth of the fact that life fits together as well as it does, but that doesn't mean that we know God's mind."[32]

BIRTH NAME: James Eugene Carrey
DATE OF BIRTH: January 17, 1962
PLACE OF BIRTH: Toronto, Canada
OCCUPATIONS: Actor, Writer, Comedian
CLAIM TO FAME: "In Living Color" (1990–1994)

JIM CARREY

In discussing his recent movie about God, Jim Carrey stated, "We've always tried to humanize Him in some way. He's probably just a shaft of light in a doorway or something like that…"[33]

He said about faith, "We're spiritual in a sense and I've always been big about faith. Everything in my life has happened for a good reason. Generally when I'm on the beam, man, it's like the blessings just come one after another, like rain. It's unbelievable."[34]

Carrey says he is more spiritual, than religious, and doesn't abide to a specific religious faith. "I've gone multi-denominational. I've studied a lot of different things and basically I don't know what God is but I know that He's at least an energy that rules all that walks the earth and I really think there are laws. There are laws and maybe they're within us. I don't know what it is, but I call that God too."[35]

Jim Carrey is very perceptive in thinking that there are "laws," and that they are within us. The Bible, our plumb line, does say that "the work of the Law" is written on our hearts, "our conscience bearing witness."[36] The Law that is being referred to is the Moral Law (the Ten Commandments). Each of us knows intuitively that it is wrong to lie, to steal, to commit adultery, etc. In fact, the word "conscience" comes from two Greek words: *con* (with) and *science* (knowledge). Whenever we lie, steal, commit adultery, etc., we do it "with knowledge" that it is wrong.

BIRTH NAME: Hugh Marston Hefner
DATE OF BIRTH: April 9, 1926
PLACE OF BIRTH: Chicago, Illinois
OCCUPATION: Publisher
CLAIM TO FAME: Founder of *Playboy* magazine

HUGH HEFNER

Hugh Hefner's life philosophy began in his youth: "I was a very idealistic, very romantic kid in a very typically Midwestern Methodist repressed home."[37] He said that he later discovered how organized religion degraded the outlooks of both men and women.

According to Hefner, "If a man has a right to find God in his own way, he has a right to go to the devil in his own way also... Religious leaders can attempt to persuade us of the correctness of their beliefs—they have this right, and indeed it is expected of them. They have no right, however, to attempt in any way to force their beliefs on others."[38]

When asked if he feared death, Hefner answered, "I'm very comfortable with the nature of life and death, and that we come to an end. What's most difficult to imagine is that those dreams and early yearnings and desires of childhood and adolescence will also disappear. But who knows? Maybe you become part of the eternal whatever."[39]

Many people think Christianity is repressive, especially when they misunderstand the teachings of the Bible. It does say, "Wives, submit to your own husbands, as to the Lord," but it also instructs, "Husbands, love your wives, just as Christ also loved the church and gave Himself for it."[40]

A man who understands that Jesus Christ sacrificed His life's blood for the Church will likewise love his wife sacrificially and passionately. He will honor her, respect her, protect, love, and cherish her as much as he does his own body, as he is instructed to do.[41] He will never say or do anything to harm or demean her. It is in this atmosphere of love and security that a wife willingly submits herself to the protective arms of her husband. She does this not because he is better than she is, but simply because this is God's order for His creation.

Those who don't believe this are rejecting the God-given formula for a successful marriage. Thinking they know best, they suffer the heartbreaking consequences of destroyed marriages and ruined lives.

The Christian ideal of marriage is not one of an authoritarian, chauvinistic male holding his cringing wife in submission like an obedient dog. Such a thought is absurd. In fact, the opposite is true. While most major religions consider women to be inferior to men, the Bible gives them a place of dignity, responsibility, honor, and unspeakable worth, expressed so clearly in Proverbs 31.

Although Hefner's name is synonymous with sexual pleasure, he had nothing to do with it. Neither did sex come about through an evolutionary process (something else we will look at later in this book). Despite those who believe religion is repressive, sex was actually a gift given by God for procreation and for pleasure. The "plumb line" says that a man should enjoy the wife of his youth. He is told to be *ravished* (enraptured) always with her love.[42] The only stipulation is that he is enraptured with *his* wife—not the woman down the street.

Those who forsake marriage, thinking they can freely enjoy sex outside its protective bonds, risk getting AIDS and numerous other sexually transmitted diseases—several of which are incurable. It is interesting to note that a man and a woman who engage in sex ten thousand times solely *within* their marriage never risk contracting any sexually transmitted disease.

One who commits fornication (from the Greek *Porneia*, "illicit sexual intercourse") takes what could lawfully be his as a gift from

God, and corrupts it. He is like a child who one night sneaks in and steals a crisp, new twenty-dollar bill from his father's wallet, not realizing that his father intended to give it to him as a gift in the morning.

BIRTH NAME: William Ray Cyrus
DATE OF BIRTH: August 25, 1961
PLACE OF BIRTH: Flatwoods, Kentucky
OCCUPATIONS: Recording Artist, Actor
CLAIM TO FAME: Hit single "Achy Breaky Heart" (1992)

BILLY RAY CYRUS

Billy Ray Cyrus said, "If you're going to stand up for Jesus, your life will be a battle between light and darkness. And for everything that God will bring into your life that represents the light, the devil, he's such a sly fox, will come at you with two times more attributes of evil...

"I made a lot of mistakes, but I was fortunate that I was brought up in a church where I heard about God's love and His forgiveness. I might have gotten a little wild, but I never left my faith. Luckily, teachings from the Bible were instilled so deep inside me that no matter how far I would stray, I'd still hear that voice that said, 'You have a purpose, you have a reason you were put on this earth, you've got to be the person God wants you to be.'"[43]

Cyrus readily admits, "By no means...am I proclaiming that I'm this perfect, religious person. I'm not all of a sudden stepping up on a pedestal and saying I'm holier than thou, because I'm not! I'm a very imperfect person," he notes, "but isn't that why God sent his son Jesus to this earth? To save sinners like me?"[44]

BIRTH NAME: Michael Joseph Jackson
DATE OF BIRTH: August 29, 1958
PLACE OF BIRTH: Gary, Indiana
OCCUPATIONS: Musician, Producer, Composer
CLAIM TO FAME: Lead singer in the Jackson Five

MICHAEL JACKSON

Most people know Michael Jackson came from a Jehovah's Witness background. He explained that his family spent Sundays "Pioneering," going door to door or making the rounds of a shopping mall, distributing *Watchtower* magazines. He remembers, "Sundays were sacred for two other reasons as I was growing up. They were both the day that I attended church and the day that I spent rehearsing my hardest. This may seem against the idea of 'rest on the Sabbath,'[45] but it was the most sacred way I could spend my time: developing the talents that God gave me."[46]

He noted, "When circumstances made it increasingly complex for me to attend [church], I was comforted by the belief that God exists in my heart, and in music and in beauty, not only in a building." Nonetheless, he admitted, "There have been times in my life when I, like everyone, has had to wonder about God's existence."[47]

We need never wonder whether or not God exists, and what's more, it has nothing to do with faith. Let me explain. Let's consider a building and ask the question, how do I know there was a builder? I can't see him, hear him, touch, taste, or smell him. Of course, the build*ing* is proof that there was a build*er*. In fact, I couldn't want better evidence that there was a builder than to have the building in front of me. I don't need "faith" to know that there was a builder. All I need is eyes that can see and a brain that works.

Likewise, when I look at a painting, how can I know that there was a painter? Again, the paint*ing* is proof positive that there was a paint*er*. I don't need "faith" to believe in a painter because I can see the clear evidence.

The same principle applies with the existence of God. When I look at creation, how can I *know* that there was a Creator? I can't see Him, hear Him, touch Him, taste Him, or smell Him. How can I know that He exists? Why, creation shows me that there is a Creator. *I couldn't want better proof that a Creator exists than to have the creation in front of me.* I don't need faith to believe in a Creator; all I need is eyes that can see and a brain that works. The Bible tells us that "since the creation of the world His invisible attributes are clearly seen, being understood by the things that are made, even His eternal power and Godhead, so that they are without excuse."[48]

If, however, I want the builder to *do* something for me, then I need to have faith in him. The same applies to God: "Without faith it is impossible to please Him, for he who comes to God must believe that He is, and that He is a rewarder of those who diligently seek Him."[49] If I want to have a relationship with God, it must be built on "trust," just as with healthy relationships we have with other human beings.

BIRTH NAME: John Joseph Nicholson
DATE OF BIRTH: April 22, 1937
PLACE OF BIRTH: Neptune, New Jersey
OCCUPATIONS: Actor, Director, Writer
CLAIM TO FAME: *One Flew Over the Cuckoo's Nest* (1975)

JACK NICHOLSON

Jack Nicholson frankly admitted, "I don't believe in God now," but added, "I can still work up an envy for someone who has faith. I can see how that could be a deeply soothing experience."[50]

It's interesting that Nicholson "can still work up an envy for someone who has faith." Most people misunderstand what faith is. It's not something that is mustered up despite overwhelming contrary evidence. Neither is it a *belief* in God's existence. I had faith *before* my conversion to Christianity, and I even prayed every night. However, my faith was an *intellectual belief* rather than what is required for someone to come to know God. Let me try to explain the difference between the two, relating it to the Christian faith, because that's my particular perspective.

A young boy was once staring at a heater, fascinated by its bright orange glow. His father saw him and warned, "Don't touch that heater, son. It may look nice, but it's hot." The boy believed him, and moved away from the heater.

Sometime later, after his father had left the room, the little boy thought, "I wonder if it really is hot." He then reached out and touched it. The second his flesh burned, he stopped *believing* it was hot; he now *knew* it was hot! He had moved out of the realm of *belief* into the realm of *experience*.

When I obeyed the Word of God, turned from my sins, and embraced Jesus Christ, I stopped merely believing. The moment I reached out and touched the heater bar of God's mercy, I moved out of *belief* into the realm of *experience*. This experience is so radical, Jesus referred to it as being "born again."

The Bible tells us that those who don't know God are spiritually dead.[51] Those who place their faith in Jesus Christ receive His life. There is a big difference between a corpse and a living, breathing human. The difference between what the Bible calls the "saved" and those who are lost is just as radical.

Those who now have God's Spirit living in them will love what He loves and desire to do His will. They will have a hunger for His Word (the Bible) and a deep love and concern for other people. The Holy Spirit also confirms in their spirit that they are now children of God.[52] Those who believe on the name of the Son of God *know* that they have eternal life.[53] This all comes with the experience of being born again.

Now suppose a heater manufacturer and a skin specialist walked into the room just after that child had burned his hand on the heater. Both assured the boy that he couldn't possibly have been burned. But all the experts, theories, and arguments in the world will not dissuade that boy, *because of his experience.* Those who have been transformed by God's power need never fear scientific or other "intellectual" arguments, because the man with an experience is not at the mercy of a man with an argument.

BIRTH NAME: Halle Maria Berry
DATE OF BIRTH: August 14, 1966
PLACE OF BIRTH: Cleveland, Ohio
OCCUPATION: Actress
CLAIM TO FAME: *Living Dolls* (1989)

HALLE BERRY

Halle Berry stated, "I know that there is a God—the God within me that's always present and will protect me. I'm not afraid to climb any mountain, because I know that I'm protected. Even if I fall and die, I'm still protected. My faith is on that level.

"I meditate and pray all the time. The faith and respect that I have in the power of God in my life is what I've used to keep myself grounded, and it has allowed me to move away from the storms that were in my life. I'm still a work in progress, but I know that as long as I stay close to God I'll be all right."[54]

BIRTH NAME: John Charles Carter
DATE OF BIRTH: October 4, 1924
PLACE OF BIRTH: Evanston, Illinois
OCCUPATION: Actor
CLAIM TO FAME: *The Ten Commandments* (1956)

CHARLTON HESTON

Charlton Heston said, "Ever since playing Moses in *The Ten Commandments* I've felt a deep, personal connection with the Bible which remains as vivid and vital today as when it was told around campfires centuries before there was any written language."[55]

One of Charlton Heston's award-winning roles was that of the title character in *Ben-Hur*. A galley slave, Judah Ben-Hur was unjustly condemned to die at the Roman oars. The ship's commander had pity on him and decided that Ben-Hur was not to be chained to the vessel as it entered battle. To ensure that slaves were committed to the cause, it was the custom of the Romans to chain them to the ship. If slaves didn't row as they should and the ship went down, they went with it. Similar to corporate America.

During battle, the ship was rammed and began to sink. Feeling the power of the will to live, the slaves began ripping at the ankle rings that coupled them to the ship. It was a graphic and dramatic scene as they drew blood in an effort to break free from their chains.

Instead of saving himself, Ben-Hur went for the guy with the keys. He overcame him, grabbed the keys, unlocked the chains, and set the captives free.

What a powerful picture of what Jesus of Nazareth did for humanity. Each of us is bound by chains to a sinking ship. Sin and death will justly take us down to the depth of hell. But there was

One who wasn't chained to sin and to death. He was without sin. The Bible says that it was not possible that death could hold Him.

When He was on the cross, Jesus was taunted to save Himself. But he didn't. Instead, He went for the guy with the keys—the one who had the power of death. The Bible says that Jesus came in the likeness of human beings "so that by his death he might destroy him who holds the power of death—that is, the devil—and free those who all their lives were held in slavery by their fear of death."[56]

Satan, the god of this world, had the power of death—until the Son of God rose from the grave. Look at Jesus' wonderful words: "I am he that lives, and was dead; and, behold, I am alive for evermore, Amen; and have the keys of hell and of death."[57]

BIRTH NAME: Maria Owings Shriver
DATE OF BIRTH: November 6, 1955
PLACE OF BIRTH: Chicago, Illinois
OCCUPATIONS: TV Host, Author, Wife of Arnold Schwarzenegger
CLAIM TO FAME: Peabody- and Emmy Award-winning Journalist

MARIA SHRIVER

In reference to a children's book she had written called *What's Heaven?*, Maria Shriver was asked, "Do you bring faith and God into this book? How do you handle those difficult topics... especially to a nonbeliever?" She answered, "Yes, I bring faith and God into the book. But, this is a book that I hope appeals to all religions. I explain death as a process of your life being over here on earth and that you go to Heaven to be with God. I talk about the soul and I try to give answers to very basic questions."[58]

Shriver, who was raised Catholic, leaves open the description of what heaven is like: "Some people believe in different kinds of heaven and have different names for it."[59]

BIRTH NAME: Leonard Simon Nimoy
DATE OF BIRTH: March 26, 1931
PLACE OF BIRTH: Boston, Massachusetts
OCCUPATIONS: Actor, Director, Producer
CLAIM TO FAME: Mr. Spock on "Star Trek"

LEONARD NIMOY

When Leonard Nimoy was asked by an interviewer if he was a religious man, he replied, "No, not particularly. I certainly don't live in a kosher home although I was raised in a kosher environment. My wife and I are affiliated with a temple...but I consider myself more spiritual than religious."[60]

This actor has a very interesting vocation. He photographs something his interviewer calls "the divine feminine." It may seem strange, but such a belief is not as uncommon as one would think.

Nimoy is honest and logical about his fascination with the female body. In reference to his artistic gifting, he admits, "I'm drawn to it. I enjoy working with it. I like it. It's something that artists have been drawn to for centuries. I enjoy it in sculpture, I enjoy it in painting. I enjoy it in the flesh."

Envisioning females as divine, or goddesses, is nothing new. In the New Testament, the apostle Paul's preaching upset some folks whose deity was a woman named Diana:

> For a certain man named Demetrius, a silversmith, who made silver shrines of Diana, brought no small profit to the craftsmen. He called them together with the workers of similar occupation, and said: "Men, you know that we have our prosperity by this trade. Moreover you see and hear that not only at Ephesus, but throughout almost all Asia, this Paul has persuaded and turned away many people, saying that they are not gods which are made with hands. So not

only is this trade of ours in danger of falling into disrepute, but also the temple of the great goddess Diana may be despised and her magnificence destroyed, whom all Asia and the world worship." Now when they heard this, they were full of wrath and cried out, saying, "Great is Diana of the Ephesians!"[61]

It is common to fashion a god in our own image. I was guilty of this. However, it is a transgression of the First and Second of the Ten Commandments: we should have no other god before the God who revealed Himself to Moses, and we should not make any image that we worship. My image of God wasn't a female one, but I did shape a god to suit myself—one that made me feel comfortable. My god was kind and good. He wasn't angry, nor did he give me any moral dictates. I was happy with him and prayed to him every night. However, my god didn't exist; he was merely a figment of my overripe imagination.

BIRTH NAME: Lisa Whelchel
DATE OF BIRTH: May 29, 1963
PLACE OF BIRTH: Littlefield, Texas
OCCUPATIONS: Actress, Singer, Author
CLAIM TO FAME: "Facts of Life" (1979–1988)

LISA WHELCHEL

Lisa Whelchel, when asked about her faith, replied that she's been a Christian since she was ten years old. After trying everything she could to deal with her son's Attention Deficit Disorder (ADD), she admitted that she called out to God. "The Lord takes us really seriously when we call upon Him, even in desperation. He began to answer me every time...and He would give me an idea."[62]

She explained the importance of teaching her children about God: "If they only do the right thing because they don't want to get in trouble, then as soon as they get out from under your covering they'll just go do what they want to do...That's why I use Scripture a lot, too; so it's not just because 'I'm the mom and I say so, it's because this is what God says about your behavior'...The goal of discipline is self-discipline, so we have to teach them that God has good reasons why He requires things from us."[63]

She describes a book she's writing that's a collection of stories from her life: "It really illustrates a really loving father/daughter relationship between my Heavenly Father and me, and how He desires to be intimately involved in the details of our lives."[64]

BIRTH NAME: Shaun Paul Cassidy
DATE OF BIRTH: September 27, 1958
PLACE OF BIRTH: Los Angeles, California
OCCUPATIONS: Actor, Writer, Musician
CLAIM TO FAME: *The Hardy Boys Mysteries* (1977–78)

SHAUN CASSIDY

Shaun Cassidy said, "More people have died in the name of religion than any war. I'm not a big fan of religion for that reason. But I am a true believer in God, and I have great faith, and I think that a spiritual connection with something is a really important part of our experience. That doesn't necessarily have anything to do with the church."[65]

BIRTH NAME: Mary Frances Reynolds
DATE OF BIRTH: April 1, 1932
PLACE OF BIRTH: El Paso, Texas
OCCUPATION: Actress
CLAIM TO FAME: *June Bride* (1948)

DEBBIE REYNOLDS

D ebbie Reynolds was asked what it was that helped her through the hard times. She replied, "My faith in the fact that I believe God's looking after me and I'm here because I have a purpose, and I feel that I should fight hard to try to survive and to try to do good for others as well as myself and my family. I live by the Ten Commandments and I believe in them, and I stay right with that."[66]

Most people think that living by the Ten Commandments is relatively easy. However, the Commandments are like the stars. From a distance stars appear to be little twinkling lights, but when viewed through a powerful telescope, we see that many are massive objects that dwarf our great earth. When we view the Ten Commandments from a distance, they seem like little lights by which we are to live, but on closer examination we see things differently. The purpose of the Ten Commandments isn't for us to have a standard by which to live. Rather, the Moral Law was given as a mirror so that we could see ourselves in truth. Think how your mirror works. It simply reflects the truth: it shows you that your face needs washing. That's what the Law does. It reveals the "dirt" of our soul, and sends us to the water of God's mercy for cleansing.

While trying to live by the Ten Commandments may sound commendable, in reality it's not. Think of it this way. A devious criminal stands guilty of serious crimes before a respected judge. The evidence reveals that the criminal is guilty of violating the law.

He even admits to his crimes, but his defense is that he is now law-abiding.

In summation, the judge looks at him and says, "You are guilty of terrible crimes. Do you want me to praise you because you are now law-abiding? I don't think so. It is only right that you obey the law, and in your doing so, you are condemned even further because you are admitting that the law you have violated is good and right."

The night of my conversion I realized I stood as a guilty criminal before a holy God. The Law's indictment against me is too large to record on this page, but here are some of the accusations. I had broken the Ninth Commandment by telling a lie. I was guilty of violating the Seventh Commandment by looking with lust. The Tenth Commandment accused me of coveting what didn't belong to me. I had failed to put God first in my life—I didn't love Him with all of my heart, soul, mind, and strength—nor did I love my neighbor as myself. As a normal human, all I was interested in was how I could please myself, rather than the God who gave me life. Instead I had made a god to suit myself—one who had no ethical dictates to give me a sense of guilt—and I parroted the Lord's Prayer nightly to the idol I had created within my mind. That god I did love, but he didn't exist; I made him up. I had also violated God's Law by being a thief, stealing apples from our neighbors. My crimes may seem trivial by human standards, but from God's perspective I was an idolatrous, lying, thieving, covetous, rebellious adulterer-at-heart. And these were just a few of my sins. The Bible says each of us has a *multitude* of transgressions.

Imagine there was someone on earth who was almost perfect. He sinned only three times a day. Perhaps a selfish thought entered his mind and he failed to love someone else as much as he loved himself. Or he failed to love God, just for a moment with all of his heart, soul, mind, and strength. Or perhaps he looked with lust, or had an envious thought or anger without cause. By sinning just three times a day, over one year he sinned against God one thousand times. Over twenty years, God has seen 20,000 of his sins, and because God is good by nature, He must bring every crime to justice.

Think now of your own standing before God. Have you been morally perfect, twenty-four hours a day, seven days a week, 365 days each year? Or are you like I was, living for yourself, guilty of a multitude of sins? Are you going to justify yourself by saying you are trying to live by the Moral Law? Don't be fooled that you're going to impress God by such a thought. You can't find any help from the Law you have already violated; all it does is call for your blood. It is an anvil for Eternal Justice. What then should you do? Simply call on the Judge for clemency. Tell Him you are guilty, and you have no justification at all for the crimes you have committed.

He has made provision to dismiss the guilty criminal, by paying his fine in full two thousand years ago on an old rugged cross. Jesus satisfied the demands of the Law for justice, then He rose from the grave, defeating death. You can be acquitted from the courtroom when you place your trust in the Savior. Once you do so, you will want to keep the Ten Commandments, not as a guilty criminal, but as a Law-abiding citizen of the Kingdom of God. Your motive is no longer one of guilt—trying to be justified by keeping the Law—but one of gratitude, because of the mercy of the Judge.

BIRTH NAME: Mel Columcille Gerard Gibson
DATE OF BIRTH: January 3, 1956
PLACE OF BIRTH: Peekskill, New York
OCCUPATIONS: Actor, Director, Producer
CLAIM TO FAME: *Mad Max* (1979)

MEL GIBSON

Mel Gibson talked about why he decided to produce *The Passion of the Christ*: "I had always believed in God, that He existed, and I was brought up to believe in a certain way. But in my middle years, I kind of drifted, and other things took center stage. At that point, I realized I needed something more if I was going to survive. A closer investigation of the Gospels, of the story, of the whole piece, was demanded of me...

"The Passion is the biggest adventure story of all time. I think it's the biggest love-story of all time; God becoming man and men killing God—if that's not action, nothing is."[67]

BIRTH NAME: Issur Danielovitch Demsky
DATE OF BIRTH: December 9, 1916
PLACE OF BIRTH: Amsterdam, New York
OCCUPATIONS: Actor, Producer, Director
CLAIM TO FAME: *Spartacus* (1960)

KIRK DOUGLAS

When asked if his health problems caused him to re-embrace Judaism, Kirk Douglas answered, "I don't think my interest in it would have come about if I hadn't been heavily reminded of mortality... But I think everybody has to come to terms with some spiritual growth. In my case, I was born a Jew, but I neglected it for sixty years, and then it was suddenly reawakened and I became a strong Jew, yet in a secular way."[68]

About the reality of sin he stated, "We are all sinners, but God always gives us a second chance. I'm a sinner who's trying to overcome my sins and be a better person." [69]

He also admitted, "I have argued with God and gotten angry with God, and I think it's permissible to do that. The only thing that is not permissible is to ignore God." Asked about the greatest thing life has taught him, Douglas replied, "That we are lucky to be alive, and that if God has given you free will, it is up to you to do something to fulfill your life and to not only work on the outside of it but to think also of what goes into it."[70]

Kirk Douglas is right: we *are* all sinners,[71] but none of us can overcome the *power* of sin. It would be easier to build a bacon burger restaurant on the Temple Mount in Jerusalem than to overcome sin. This is because the Bible speaks of being a slave to sin and being held captive by its power.[72]

Each of us is drawn to sin as a moth to a flame—and the penalty of sin is death. Even if we were able to overcome a particular sin, our past sins demand payment in the same way that civil law demands a guilty criminal's blood. Sin is something that has already been dealt with by God. Only by turning from our sins and trusting in Christ can we overcome the power of sin and death.[73]

BIRTH NAME: John Tesh
DATE OF BIRTH: July 9, 1952
PLACE OF BIRTH: Long Island, New York
OCCUPATIONS: Musician, TV/Radio Host
CLAIM TO FAME: Co-host of "Entertainment Tonight" (1986–1996)

JOHN TESH

John Tesh said, "You'll find a lot of people who don't want to be honest about their faith on their TV shows, but they're fine for you to come on and do it." He said of his childhood, "Our whole lives revolved around the church. We were there three days a week and I went to church camp every summer." Yet, he admitted, "I had no relationship with Christ. I had a relationship with the idea of going to church. You read hymn number whatever, looked up Scripture, stood up, sat down, and that was it."[74]

One day he heard a well-known preacher deliver a message about the need for Christian men to "come out of the closet." When he was challenged to be more public about his faith, he realized, "When you get a little older you think, 'What's going to be on my tombstone?' I really had nothing. That's when I decided to be a little more honest about my faith."[75]

BIRTH NAME: Laurence Fishburne III
DATE OF BIRTH: July 30, 1961
PLACE OF BIRTH: Augusta, Georgia
OCCUPATIONS: Actor, Director, Producer
CLAIM TO FAME: *Apocalypse Now* (1979)

LAURENCE FISHBURNE

W hen he was asked if he had something in life "that you really believe in," Laurence Fishburne said, "I have this unshakeable faith. I believe in myself, I believe in God. I had two times in my life where I wanted to give up everything I worked for, but God gave me a job. I believe in my children. I believe in human beings. I believe in the goodness that is in human beings. I believe in many, many things that I cannot prove. I believe that there's the world of the seen and the world of the unseen."[76]

BIRTH NAME: Ernestine Jane Geraldine Russell
DATE OF BIRTH: June 21, 1921
PLACE OF BIRTH: Bemidji, Minnesota
OCCUPATION: Actress
CLAIM TO FAME: *The Outlaw* (1943)

JANE RUSSELL

I n commenting about Mel Gibson's movie *The Passion of the Christ*, Jane Russell said, "I hope that *The Passion of the Christ* gets to at least a billion." She added some advice to Hollywood:

"I hope now that the producers are getting caught on to what people really want to see...I hope they will see that you can make more money by far by making family films with Judeo-Christian background."[77]

At age 81, Russell appeared on a panel discussion in which she stated, "My son said, 'Mother, you can't say the word bigot because that has to do with nationalities and things.' I said, 'No darling, it's a verb. It means I can't stand these people who are trying to take the Ten Commandments off the wall, take prayer out of school and...take prayer out of football games.' It's too ridiculous. The Lord put this country together or we wouldn't be like we are."[78]

BIRTH NAME: Peter Charles Archibald Ewart Jennings
DATE OF BIRTH: July 29, 1938
PLACE OF BIRTH: Toronto, Canada
OCCUPATIONS: News Anchorman, Actor
CLAIM TO FAME: Anchor of ABC's "World News Tonight"

PETER JENNINGS

Raised an Anglican, Peter Jennings said he is a practicing Christian, yet he has gone through a period of seeking to understand "how strong or what are the connections I have to God." In answer to a question about prayer, Jennings candidly replied, "Yes. I have prayed. But I am quick to qualify that I was brought up—I was taught to pray as a child...But your question should be, 'When you pray, do you know what you are doing?' And that question I won't answer." Jennings continued, "I don't want to be identified as someone who, at any given moment in their life, gets down on his knees and seeks whatever."[79]

In discussing a television program he was producing about the life of Jesus, he said, "By simply looking at the man, and by looking at it in the context of the first century, are you undermining the very notion that He is the Son of God and He did die for *our* sins? That's a tough one."[80]

Actually, it isn't that tough. In fact, the intellectual dilemma comes when we do try to separate the Man Jesus from the claim that He was the Son of God, sent to "die for *our* sins." Jesus was born through the womb of a woman; he had a mother. However, the biblical claim is that He had no earthly father. His mother was a virgin when He was conceived *of the Holy Spirit*.[81] He walked on earth as a human being, but He claimed that He was pre-existent and that He "came down from heaven."[82] He became tired, hungry, and thirsty like the rest of us, yet He was able to miraculously multiply food and feed multitudes. That may be a little hard to swallow for some, but that is the historical record of Scripture. If that testimony can't be relied upon, how can we believe *anything* in the Bible? Or do we only believe what we consider believable?

If we think the record of His virgin birth was fabricated, how can we believe that He was born in Nazareth, that his mother was named Mary, or that He even existed at all?

BIRTH NAME: Gladys Leeman
DATE OF BIRTH: January 12, 1955
PLACE OF BIRTH: Wichita, Kansas
OCCUPATIONS: Actress, Producer
CLAIM TO FAME: "Cheers" (1987–1993)

KIRSTIE ALLEY

Kirstie Alley spoke of her faith in Scientology: "I wanted some solutions. It made sense to me that if you had a flat tire you got a new tire. I thought there has to be something that can get rid of problems and in *Dianetics* it tells you how to get rid of painful emotions and physical pain from the past, and I just thought, wow, that's what I want; I want it to be gone."[83]

BIRTH NAME: Al Franken
DATE OF BIRTH: May 21, 1951
PLACE OF BIRTH: New York City, New York
OCCUPATIONS: Actor, Comedian, Author, Producer,
Radio Talk Show Host
CLAIM TO FAME: "Saturday Night Live" (1977–80, 1986–95)

AL FRANKEN

Al Franken, well-known comedian and outspoken political activist, is also forthright about faith. When asked about the existence of hell, he simply said, "I think hell exists on earth. It's a psychological state or it can be a physical state. People who have severe mental illness are in hell. People who have lost a loved one are in hell. I think there are all kinds of different hells. It's not a place you go to after you die."[84]

Asked to describe his spiritual life, Franken stated, "My spiritual life is...sometimes I have access to it and sometimes I don't... [That] means when I'm in a more spiritual place than when I'm ...reacting maybe more out of non spiritual reasons—either anger or ambition or lust, those kinds of things. None of those are necessarily bad."[85]

It seems odd that he adamantly states "it's not a place you go to after you die," because his next sentence is: "I don't know what happens to you after you die."[86]

Perhaps he would be safer to say with the popular '60s rock group Blood, Sweat and Tears, "We say that there is no heaven, and *pray* that there is no hell..."

For those who believe hell exists on earth, I would ask an important question. If there were a place of punishment called "hell," would they want to be warned about it? If there were even a remote possibility that they could end up there, would they want to know how it could be avoided? I'm sure any thinking person would.

This logic may help. What is your concept of God? Do you think He is good or evil? Most of us would say that God is good. With that understanding in mind, consider this question: Should God punish those who rape and murder? Let's be specific. A man kidnaps a pretty teenage girl and keeps her in chains as a sex slave for two weeks. Then to her horror he coldly explains that he's going to have to kill her because she has seen his face and could identify him. With tears streaming down her cheeks, she desperately pleads for her life, swearing that she won't identify him. She promises to forget *everything*.

Her pleas are to no avail. He mercilessly slits her throat and decapitates her. He then systematically cuts up her body, dissolves it in an acid bath, and flushes the remains through the sewage system. With no body, there is no evidence to convict him of any crime. His confidence that he'll never be caught is understandable—this was his seventh victim. He had the expertise to ensure that he didn't leave a single hair or a drop of blood. He could commit the perfect crime.

Should God bring this man to justice? This vicious murderer has completely escaped *man's* justice, so should God eventually punish him? Some might argue that his guilt would be punishment enough, but let's follow that logic for a moment.

If that were true, why do we have court systems? Why do we bother punishing a bank robber or rapist, if his own guilty feelings are punishment enough?

We go to great lengths to punish wrongdoing, often spending *millions* of dollars to bring even one murderer to justice. It is our desire for justice that separates us from the animals. Animals don't set up court systems to punish injustice. Humans are *moral* beings because we have been made in God's image. We are moral because He is moral.

God is good, so He must therefore bring criminals to justice. Someone who is good cannot allow injustice to go unpunished.

The serial killer who committed the "perfect crime" isn't alone. In the last twenty years in the U.S. approximately 200,000 people were murdered. Only 50 percent of those homicide cases were solved, meaning approximately 100,000 killers got away with murder. They viciously strangled, shot, drowned, poisoned, or stabbed another human being, and were never brought to justice! Since God is good, He should be more than concerned; He should be outraged.

Therefore it is reasonable to conclude that God will bring murderers to justice. Is He good enough to also bring rapists to justice? Of course. How about thieves? Adulterers? Liars? The depth of His justice will be in direct proportion to His goodness. If God is absolutely good, He will require absolute justice. If He didn't, He would be corrupt.

Here is another interesting question. Do you have a conscience? What does it do for you? It tells you right from wrong. Was that knowledge learned or were you born with it? If you think it was learned, consider this scenario.

A twenty-year-old man is found guilty of a brutal murder. The defense maintained that the man had been isolated since birth from all human interaction, so no one had taught him right from wrong. Not a soul. He had no moral instruction. Zip.

In passing sentence is the judge going to say, "You are found guilty of murder, but because you were never taught right from wrong I will therefore dismiss your case"? No good judge would ever say that! If he did, he would be a criminal himself. He is obligated to carry out the demands of the law. The guilty man is without excuse—every human being knows it's wrong to murder because he has been *born* with a conscience.

None of us can plead, "I didn't know right from wrong!" as a defense when we stand before God. The plumb line tells us that He has given "light" to every man and woman. We all have an innate knowledge of right and wrong.

So if God is good, it is reasonable to conclude that there is going to be a Day when He will punish murderers and rapists. Because God is so good and His justice will be so thorough, He will also punish thieves, adulterers, idolaters, and all liars. And because we each have a conscience, anyone who is proven guilty on that Day cannot plead moral ignorance. As in the movies, the evil guys get what's coming to them...and the prison that God has for them is a place of punishment called "hell."

BIRTH NAME: Benjamin Geza Affleck
DATE OF BIRTH: August 15, 1972
PLACE OF BIRTH: Berkeley, California
OCCUPATION: Actor
CLAIM TO FAME: *Good Will Hunting* (1997)

BEN AFFLECK

In answer to the question, "What do you do spiritually to stand grounded and focused in the business?" Ben Affleck said, "You know I know a lot of people do yoga, and a lot of eastern religions and practices have become popular here, and that's something I have not really gotten very involved with. I have my own spirituality which is of Western Christian spirituality that is effective for me.

"I think what's not so important is the brand of spirituality but that you have some sense of, some humbling sense of power larger than yourself and that the relative insignificance of man in face of the greater universe. And so I have some ways in which I keep in touch with that."[87]

BIRTH NAME: Nicholas King Nolte
DATE OF BIRTH: February 8, 1941
PLACE OF BIRTH: Omaha, Nebraska
OCCUPATIONS: Actor, Model, Producer
CLAIM TO FAME: *Return to Macon County* (1975)

NICK NOLTE

Nick Nolte confided, "I have difficulty with God and with beliefs. You have to question. If God created man in his image, what kind of image is God?"[88]

That is an interesting question. The Bible does say that God created man in His own image and likeness. Does that mean that God is like man, with all his weaknesses and sins? No. It means God created man unique in that he was, as we have seen, a moral being with a sense of justice and truth. However, we live in a "fallen" state, in which Adam and Eve's disobedience (sin) brought corruption and death to mankind. This is the Fall spoken of in the Book of Genesis.

We can see the results of the Fall in daily life: hurricanes, tornadoes, floods, droughts, and earthquakes kill tens of thousands of people each year. Multitudes endure crippling diseases, endless suffering, and unspeakable pain. Many credit a heartless Mother Nature for giving us all this grief. They fail to consider that "Mother Nature" has a Senior Partner—Father God. However, if God is responsible for all this heartache, that presents an interesting dilemma. If God is an "all-loving" Father figure, as we are so often told He is, we seem to have three choices: 1) God blew it when He made everything (He's creative but incompetent); 2) God is a tyrant, who gets His kicks from seeing people crushed by earthquakes and kids die of leukemia; 3) Or something between God and man is radically wrong.

These are our only choices...and those who take time to consider the evidence will lean toward number three. Something between man and God *is* radically wrong, and the Scriptures tell us what it is.

Because we live in a fallen state, God is not the jovial father figure many make Him out to be; He is not our friend. There is a war going on and we are in a state of hostility toward Him. We are told that mankind is an enemy of God in his mind through wicked works.[89] That's not too hard to see. Man is continually committing violent acts such as murder and rape, lying, stealing, etc., as the daily news confirms. He uses God's name as a curse word, while Mother Nature gets the glory for His creation—unless there's a horrible disaster; then man calls that "an act of God."

So when you hear that we are made in God's image, remember that was *before* the Fall in Genesis, when man's choice to sin corrupted human nature.

BIRTH NAME: Eldred Gregory Peck
DATE OF BIRTH: April 5, 1916
PLACE OF BIRTH: La Jolla, California
DATE OF DEATH: June 12, 2003
OCCUPATION: Actor
CLAIM TO FAME: *Days of Glory* (1944)

GREGORY PECK

Gregory Peck said, "Faith is a powerful force. To me it's been like an anchor to windward, and something that's seen me through troubled times and some personal tragedies, and through the good times and the success and the happy times as well. Faith gives you an inner strength and a sense of balance and perspective in life."[90]

When asked if he believed that there is a master plan and planner, he replied, "Oh, yes I do. I don't think anyone who ever lived has not at some time or other pondered and speculated on the mystery and the meaning of life. There has to be a master plan and a master planner. I like to remember that Albert Einstein, one of the greatest intellects in human history said that the only possible explanation for the existence of the universe is divine creation..."[91]

He added, "I've always loved the Bible...Reading it all again from start to finish and becoming a Bible student again has truly enriched my life. There's so much wisdom and so much truth, so much poetry, and so many beautiful passages, and the drama in the life and death of Christ, and in the travels and teachings of His apostles and disciples." [92]

BIRTH NAME: Robert Selden Duvall
DATE OF BIRTH: January 5, 1931
PLACE OF BIRTH: San Diego, California
OCCUPATIONS: Actor, Director, Writer, Producer
CLAIM TO FAME: *To Kill a Mockingbird* (1962)

ROBERT DUVALL

Robert Duvall stated, "If you talk about Jesus in everyday conversation in New York City or the North you're perceived as a nut, but if you do it in the South or rural America it's totally acceptable...If people want to talk about God or whatever that's their prerogative. I believe in a higher power and that's my own belief."[93]

He elaborated on his beliefs in another interview: "I just have my own way of believing and praying and contemplating...We're going to be judged one day. All I can say is that I believe in one God and Jesus Christ. I do believe that. Maybe not the way everybody does, but I have my own way. It's a private thing and I believe in that special uniqueness."[94]

Asked if he had ever had a personal experience that transformed his life or perspective in any way, Duvall replied, "Not quite like that. It's been a continuing thing. I think the experience of being reborn is a very personal experience. To standardize it is very difficult. Religion attempts to standardize it. But I find no place in the Bible where it's standardized. Being reborn on a daily basis throughout my life is the thing. No one has the definitive answer."[95]

Actually, because Jesus said being born again is essential to entering heaven, the Bible clearly explains about this crucial experience. We are told that we are dead in our sins, but the moment we turn from them and place our faith in the Savior, we pass from death to life.[96] We go from being spiritually dead to spiritually alive; our mortal nature puts on immortality. Just as the physical birth is a one-time event, so is the spiritual birth.

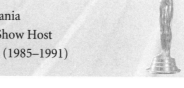

BIRTH NAME: Dennis Miller
DATE OF BIRTH: November 3, 1953
PLACE OF BIRTH: Philadelphia, Pennsylvania
OCCUPATIONS: Comedian, Actor, Talk Show Host
CLAIM TO FAME: "Saturday Night Live" (1985–1991)

DENNIS MILLER

Dennis Miller explained the philosophy that helps keep him grounded: "Show business is a freakish break. It's an amazing confluence of events that affords you a life for which you should hit your knees every night and thank God that you've been blessed to be given."[97]

Miller added, "In this messed up world, I like seeing my President pray. I don't think a person can get answers out of books anymore. This is an infinitely complex world and at some point one has to have faith in one's religion. I find it endearing that President Bush prays to God and that he's not an agnostic or an atheist. I'm glad there's someone higher that he has to answer to."[98]

BIRTH NAME: Gretchen Michaela Young
DATE OF BIRTH: January 6, 1913
PLACE OF BIRTH: Salt Lake City, Utah
DATE OF DEATH: August 12, 2000
OCCUPATION: Actress
CLAIM TO FAME: *Naughty But Nice* (1927)

LORETTA YOUNG

oretta Young, a Catholic, said, "I believe that a life without religion is, truly, an impoverished existence. I believe in the efficacy of prayer and I have a deep and sorrowful sympathy for one who is without faith. I believe our Father answers every prayer—all prayers—with His matchless, inscrutable wisdom, with infinite compassion and with love. I believe in that simple acknowledgment of God's dominion over me and my needs, The Lord's Prayer."[99]

Asked by a friend whether she believed there was anything after this life, Young replied, "Oh, I'll say. That's why to me every single solitary moment is so important. What I do here is going to decide whether I go to heaven or hell. And when I was 16 I decided I was not going to go to hell. And you can decide that. You may boo-boo 10 times a day. That's why we have confession. As long as you're sincere and trying to break the habits."[100]

It is tragic that so many misunderstand the place of repentance. When we commit a sin, our conscience does its duty and accuses us of wrongdoing. Many who listen to their conscience go to God and confess that they have sinned, thinking that their sorrow and reluctance to sin again has purchased their forgiveness. But that doesn't work even in a civil court, let alone with God. If a man commits a crime for which there is a $50,000 fine, no judge is going to dismiss the case simply because the criminal is sorry that he did wrong and says he won't commit the crime again. He *should* be sorry that he has done wrong, and of course he shouldn't commit the crime again.

If, however, the $50,000 fine is paid in full, then the judge has legal grounds to dismiss the case. The Bible tells us that eternal salvation comes, not by repentance alone, but by repentance coupled with faith in Jesus' payment of our fine on the cross. The last words uttered by Jesus of Nazareth were, "It is finished!" In other words, "The debt has been paid in full!"[101] That's why the Bible speaks of the necessity of "repentance toward God and faith toward our Lord Jesus Christ."[102]

BIRTH NAME: James Maitland Stewart
DATE OF BIRTH: May 20, 1908
PLACE OF BIRTH: Indiana, Pennsylvania
DATE OF DEATH: July 2, 1997
OCCUPATION: Actor
CLAIM TO FAME: *Mr. Smith Goes to Washington* (1936)

JIMMY STEWART

At a Boy Scout banquet held in his honor, Jimmy Stewart remarked about the Scout Oath ("On my honor I will do my best to do my duty to God and my country and to obey the Scout law; to help other people at all times; to keep myself physically strong, mentally awake, and morally straight"). He explained that he learned its forty words as a very young man, and they have stayed with him through a lifetime. He stated: "*Honor* means worth, and has been known to escalate to reverence and higher to veneration. We honor the Lord...

"*Duty to God*—means a lot more than saying a prayer every time you need a favor. A lot more. Duty to God is simply that voluntary gesture you must make and remake a million times in your lifetime as a statement of your recognition that there is Someone above this universe who watches over this universe and to whom each of us is a favorite son. Duty to God is a lifetime thank-you note our hearts send out in appreciation for the life that has been loaned to us here on earth."[103]

BIRTH NAME: William Bradley Pitt
DATE OF BIRTH: December 18, 1964
PLACE OF BIRTH: Shawnee, Oklahoma
OCCUPATION: Actor
CLAIM TO FAME: *Thelma and Louise* (1991)

BRAD PITT

B rad Pitt was a choirboy as he was growing up, and his father taught him and his siblings "to be respectable, churchgoing folk." Raised with "a strong Baptist faith,"[104] Pitt shared his spiritual beliefs in the following interview:

There is one subject [Pitt] refers to time and time again, and that is religion. "I would call it oppression," he says, "because it stifles any kind of personal individual freedom. I dealt with a lot of that, and my family would diametrically disagree with me on all of that."

It's only when we later drift into an unlikely debate about one of the New Testament parables that I realize just how different a kind of God Pitt grew up with. To him, the parable of the prodigal son is an authoritarian tale told to keep people in line. "This," he explains, "is a story which says, if you go out and try to find your own voice and find what works for you and what makes sense for you, then you are going to be destroyed and you will be humbled and you will not be alive again until you come home to the father's ways."[105]

You may not be familiar with the story Jesus told of the Prodigal Son, so let's take a moment to consider what it says. The Prodigal asked his father for his inheritance, then went into a far country and spent all his cash on parties and prostitutes. He enjoyed "the pleasures of sin." But after a famine hit the land, the only job he could get was feeding pigs. When he became so hungry that he was desiring the food that the pigs were eating, he "came to himself"— he came to his senses. Realizing that even his father's servants had it better than he did, he decided to return to his father and say, "Father, I have sinned against heaven and in your sight. Take me on as a hired servant." So he got up out of the pigsty and went back to his father.

The father was looking for his son's return, and the Bible says that "he saw him while he was yet a great way off." The father ran to him, fell upon him, kissed him, and rejoiced that his beloved son had returned. He freely forgave him and returned him to his former state.

That's a picture of you and me. We desire pig food. Our appetites are unclean in God's sight. That may sound offensive, but consider what we crave. Think for a moment of the contents of the average soap opera—adultery, jealously, lust, fornication, gossip, and greed. Or the average modern movie. To be successful in today's market it must have violence, profanity, sex, and graphic murder, preferably in slow motion. Look at the covers of magazines in bookstores and supermarkets. They are "soft-core" pornography, which a few years ago was considered hard-core and hidden from young eyes. Think of video games that kids crave—they are extremely violent and sexually perverted. Think of rock music, with its explicit sexuality, its blasphemy, and its dark side. Consider the Internet's multi-billion dollar hard-core porn industry, or how the average person uses unclean words in daily speech, without a second thought. Life in the pigsty is normal, natural, and completely acceptable.

And I have touched only the tip of the cold iceberg of humanity's sins. God actually sees our thought-life and the secret sins we hide from others. He also sees our transgressions from the perspective of absolute and pure holiness. Who can argue that our appetites are not unclean in His sight?

But despite the unclean nature of our appetites, Jesus' story of the Prodigal Son is a positive and wonderful story of God's love. If we will come to our senses and admit that our appetites are unclean, and then leave the pigsty, God will meet us halfway.

Just as the prodigal "came to himself" and sanity returned to his sin-soaked mind, take a minute to think of your desires and sins, and consider where they will take you. Ask yourself, "Which is better? Heaven or hell—death or life?" It shouldn't take long to decide. Don't try to compare yourself to others in the pigsty. Think of God's holiness and compare yourself to His Law. Is your thought-life pure? Have you loved God above all else? He gave you life. Have you loved your neighbor as much as you love yourself, as you have been commanded to? Has lust entered your heart? Have you ever hated someone, or been guilty of gossip? If your conscience is tender, it will remind you of the sins of your youth—sins that God sees as if they were committed yesterday. What will happen to you on Judgment Day? Rather than trying to justify yourself, bow your head before your Creator and simply say, "God be merciful to me, a sinner." And the wonderful thing is that God is rich in mercy to all who call upon Him.

BIRTH NAME: Charles Spencer Chaplin
DATE OF BIRTH: April 16, 1889
PLACE OF BIRTH: London, England
DATE OF DEATH: December 25, 1977
OCCUPATION: Actor
CLAIM TO FAME: Known as "The Little Tramp"

CHARLIE CHAPLIN

Charlie Chaplin stated plainly, "By simple common sense I don't believe in God..."[106]

However, in his later years, Chaplin did spell out his core beliefs: "As I grow older I am becoming more preoccupied with faith... To deny faith is to refute oneself and the spirit that generates all our creative forces. My faith is in the unknown, in all that we do not understand by reason; I believe that what is beyond our comprehension is a simple fact in other dimensions, and that in the realm of the unknown there is an infinite power for good."[107]

BIRTH NAME: John Winston Lennon
DATE OF BIRTH: October 9, 1940
PLACE OF BIRTH: Liverpool, England
DATE OF DEATH: December 8, 1980
OCCUPATIONS: Actor, Musician
CLAIM TO FAME: The Beatles

JOHN LENNON

In 1977, John Lennon made a short-lived profession of faith in Jesus Christ after watching television evangelists, and he began using expressions like "Praise the Lord" and "Thank you, Jesus."

He also attended some church services and wrote a never-released song titled "You Saved My Soul." He took his son, Sean, to a Christian theater performance, and he called "The 700 Club" help line to request prayer for his troubled marriage. He even tried to get Yoko Ono interested in Christianity.[108]

John Lennon's Christian profession lasted only a few weeks. When two missionaries confronted him with fundamental doctrines of the Bible such as the deity of Christ and a literal Fall, he rejected these.[109]

According to two books on his life, Lennon's final years were dictated by astrologers, numerologists, clairvoyants, psychics, herbalists, and tarot-card readers. In interviews shortly before his death, Lennon said his beliefs could be described as "Zen Christian, Zen pagan, Zen Marxist" or nothing at all.[110]

When asked earlier about the popularity of the Beatles, he said, "Everyone always talks about a good thing coming to an end, as if life was over...The game isn't over yet. Everyone talks in terms of the last record or the last Beatles concert—but, God willing, there are another 40 years of productivity to go."[111]

Shortly after this interview, John Lennon was tragically shot to death outside his apartment building in New York City. He was 40 years old.

Despite the unpredictability of life, if we are involved in a serious accident or learn that we have a terminal disease, we often predictably say, "I never thought this would happen to me." Tragedy and death are things that happen to other people, not us. But death is the ultimate, inevitable, and universal intrusion.

John Lennon thought he had another 40 years. He even used the words "God willing" when referring to his life, something the Bible tells each of us to do: "You ought to say, 'If the Lord wills, we shall live and do this or that.'"[112] We have tomorrow only if God is willing to give it to us. The only thing we can guarantee about our lives is that we have the current breath going into our lungs. We cannot guarantee another breath. That comes with the permission of our Creator. That's why we shouldn't put off making peace with God. We should do that today.

Every 24 hours more than 150,000 people die.[113] No doubt many of those who have gone before us are saying, "I never thought this would happen to me." So think seriously about the issues of life and death. If you don't acknowledge your mortality, you won't do anything about it.

Because I have placed my faith in Jesus Christ, the greatest joy in my life is the knowledge that death has no dominion over me. I know that I have everlasting life, and I can pass that knowledge on to others. We will look more closely at this subject later in this book.

BIRTH NAME: Walter Elias Disney
DATE OF BIRTH: December 5, 1901
PLACE OF BIRTH: Chicago, Illinois
DATE OF DEATH: December 15, 1966
OCCUPATIONS: Animator, Producer
CLAIM TO FAME: *Steamboat Willie* (1928)

WALT DISNEY

While growing up Walt Disney attended a Congregational church, where he learned "the efficacy of religion...how it helps us immeasurably to meet the trial and stress of life and keeps us attuned to the Divine inspiration."[114]

Regarding the role of religion and prayer in his life, Disney wrote: "In these days of world tensions, when the faith of men is being tested as never before, I am personally thankful that my parents taught me at a very early age to have a strong personal belief and reliance in the power of prayer for Divine inspiration...

"My own concept of prayer is not a plea for special favors, nor as a quick palliation for wrongs knowingly committed. A prayer, it seems to me, implies a promise as well as a request; at the highest level, prayer not only is a supplication for strength and guidance, but also becomes an affirmation of life and thus a reverent praise of God."[115]

"I have watched constantly that in our movie work the highest moral and spiritual standards are upheld...This religious concern for the form and content of our films goes back 40 years...Thus, whatever success I have had in bringing clean, informative entertainment to people of all ages, I attribute in great part to my Congregational upbringing and lifelong habit of prayer."[116]

BIRTH NAME: Shirley MacLean Beaty
DATE OF BIRTH: April 24, 1934
PLACE OF BIRTH: Richmond, Virginia
OCCUPATIONS: Actress, Writer, Musician, Model
CLAIM TO FAME: *Terms of Endearment* (1983)

SHIRLEY MACLAINE

In commenting on what she thought would happen in the future, Shirley MacLaine said, "I think we are going to go through a lot of climatic changes. I think we are going to deal more and more on a realistic basis about sightings of our space brothers and sisters...We need to understand that we are all children of God, with the notion of God being more spiritual than religious."[117]

She further explains her views: "I believe our spirit is an energy that lives forever. I believe we are spiritual beings that use a vehicle called a body to contain the spirit energy from life to life. I believe that when we have shed a physical body, our spirit can re-visit the physical plane of existence."[118]

MacLaine's website reveals that she is convinced of the philosophy of reincarnation. It says, "Reincarnation is a subject that has long been a staple in Eastern beliefs and has been gaining more acceptance in the West over the past two decades. Many people in

Western countries are beginning to state that the concept of physical life after death is not a contradiction to their views of Christianity. In fact, some point to the Bible as a reference."[119] She then quotes Psalm 90:3–6:

> Thou turnest man to destruction; and sayest, Return, ye children of men. For a thousand years in thy sight are but as yesterday when it is past, and as a watch in the night. Thou carriest them away as with a flood; they are as a sleep; in the morning they are like grass which groweth up. In the morning it florisheth, and groweth up; in the evening it is cut down and withereth. (KJV)

While it is rather difficult to find reincarnation in those verses (they are speaking of the fleeting nature of life), reincarnation *has* been gaining more acceptance in the West over the past two decades. To many, Eastern religions offer a sense of romantic mysticism. Those people would likely be surprised to learn that India's 220 million cows are worshiped by Hindus as the supreme givers of life (God). The cow's hooves are bathed during religious ceremonies. Their urine, considered holy, is used to anoint believers, and its dung is applied to the skin of the faithful in religious rituals. Hindus believe that all the gods inhabit some part of the cow's body.

MacLaine's beliefs may not encompass the thought that cows are divine, but she does believe in the divinity of people: "We are all God! People don't need an arbiter... We are all capable of going straight to God. But until you look deeper into the divinity of yourself, you may invest in a preacher, priest, whoever. Look, you know you're a child of God. You know everything in you is divine. Jesus taught us, the kingdom of heaven is within. It is."[120]

It is common for people to believe that each of us is "a child of God." However, this cannot be supported by the New Testament. While every human being has been created by God and we are therefore His *creation*, the Scriptures make it very clear that we are not all His children. Jesus said that if we were God's children, we would do the works of God. We are informed that there is a "spirit" that works in the "sons of disobedience."[121] This isn't exactly flattering to the human race, but it can certainly be fully supported by checking the daily news or by looking at popular entertainment at your local video store. Both are filled with unending violence, adultery, rape, murder, greed, hatred, and corruption.

We are *born* with a sinful and sin-loving nature. To verify this, consider whether you have to teach a child to lie, be greedy, or be selfish. These attitudes come naturally to children because they are part of our fallen, sinful nature. That is why we need to be born again.[122] The moment that happens, we become children of God and we then have the right to call Him "Father."[123]

BIRTH NAME: Janet Damita Jo Jackson
DATE OF BIRTH: May 16, 1966
PLACE OF BIRTH: Gary, Indiana
OCCUPATIONS: Actress, Musician
CLAIM TO FAME: Album *Control* (1986)

JANET JACKSON

When asked if there was a point in her life where she consciously decided to change her music, Janet Jackson answered, "My music didn't consciously evolve… Whatever is going on in my life is what you see. The only things you have control over are the decisions you make. God's the only one who has control over people's lives."[124]

She's very right about that, although many people would disagree with her. Most of us like to think that we have control over our own destiny, but consider how much control we have over our body. We are subject to involuntary yawning, sneezing, breathing, swallowing, sleeping, salivating, dreaming, blinking, and thinking.

We can't stop our brain from feeding itself with subconscious thoughts. We can't even control hair and nail growth. We automatically do these things, irrespective of our will. God has set our body in motion and there is little we can do about it.

We also have minimal control over our daily bodily functions. Our kidneys, bladder, intestines, heart, liver, lungs, etc., work independently of our will. It is therefore ludicrous to say that we control our destiny, when we can't control our own body.

We even have trouble *predicting* the future—such as the stock market, political outcomes, earthquakes, and even the weather. We do, however, have the ability to accurately predict our own mortality. Of that we can be sure.

BIRTH NAME: Madonna Louise Veronica Ciccone
DATE OF BIRTH: August 16, 1958
PLACE OF BIRTH: Bay City, Michigan
OCCUPATIONS: Singer, Actress
CLAIM TO FAME: Hit album *Like a Virgin* (1984)

MADONNA

Madonna was asked, "You believe in God?" to which she replied, "Absolutely."[125]

Several years ago, Madonna began studying Kabbalah, a Jewish mystical tradition based on spiritual laws of the universe. She explains, "Kabbalah helped me understand that there is a bigger picture and that being well-intentioned is great, but if you don't live your life according to the laws of the universe, you bring chaos into your life." Raised Catholic, Madonna stated, "I don't think there's anything wrong with the teachings of Jesus, but I am suspicious of organized religion. Kabbalah has nothing to do with organized religion. It's not judgmental. It's a manual for living."[126]

Some people consider Christianity to be judgmental, in that it labels certain actions and even thoughts as immoral, and it is exclusive. At Christianity's core is its claim that there is only one way for people to find forgiveness of sins. However, it seems that those who view Christianity as intolerant and judgmental should be more tolerant toward it, and not have a judgmental attitude about its exclusive nature.

Their thinking is often based on the incorrect notion that people will go to hell "because they don't believe in Jesus," or that those who have never heard of Jesus Christ will be condemned. This makes no sense at all. It seems unreasonable that God would eternally damn anyone just for *not believing* something. However, it makes more sense in the light of the following thought.

If a man jumps out of a plane without a parachute, he will perish because he transgressed the law of gravity. Had he put on a parachute, he would have been saved. In one sense, he perished because he didn't put on the parachute. But the *primary* reason he died was because he broke the law of gravity.

If a man refuses to trust in Jesus Christ when he passes through the door of death, he will perish. This isn't because he refused to trust in the Savior, but *primarily* because he transgressed the Law of God. Had he "put on the Lord Jesus Christ,"[127] he would have been saved; but because he refused to repent, he will suffer the full consequences of his sin. Sin is not "failing to believe in Jesus." Sin is "transgression of the Law."[128]

So Madonna was correct in pointing out, "If you don't live your life according to the laws of the universe, you bring chaos into your life"—both this one, and the life to come.

She also candidly admitted, "The only thing that matters is the state of our soul, and that's very hard because I'm in the entertainment business, which is completely based on illusion and physical things. Any success I have is a manifestation of God. It's my ego that wants to claim ownership. It's hubris, arrogance and greed."[129]

BIRTH NAME: Katherine Anne Couric
DATE OF BIRTH: January 7, 1957
PLACE OF BIRTH: Arlington, Virginia
OCCUPATION: Broadcast Journalist
CLAIM TO FAME: Co-anchor "Today" Show (1991–present)

KATIE COURIC

In recent years Katie Couric tragically lost her husband and her sister to cancer. When asked, "Do you find strength in faith?" she replied, "I was raised a Presbyterian. I think my faith has been tested. For a period I was really angry. But I'm coming back to the fold. I go to church, which gives me a moment to be contemplative and to take stock. I admire people who have a deep, abiding faith. But I think it's hard when something terrible happens, and you can't understand why a benevolent God would allow it. There's so much suffering."[130]

While suffering often mystifies us, God has given us a strong consolation to help us overcome the pain. It *is* faith, but it is one that trusts in the promises of God—and when it comes to suffering, let's zero in on one specific promise. It's in Paul's letter to the Romans:

> "We know that all things work together for good to those who love God, to those who are the called according to His purpose."[131]

This promise says that if we have aligned ourselves with the will of God (by turning from sin, being born again, and trusting in the Savior), whatever comes our way comes only by the permissive will of God. Some terrible circumstance may not be in His perfect will, but it is in His *permissive* will. That means that God doesn't *send* the particular suffering, but He (in His infinite wisdom) allows it to happen. This is a principle dealt with in the Book of Job. The pain is still very real, but God promises to work the situation out for good.

A great preacher named Charles Spurgeon said, "Faith may swim, where reason may only paddle." This is so true. The more you trust God in adversity, the more peace you will have in the storm. This is evidently seen when Jesus *slept* in a boat while He was in a violent storm. Peter also slept soundly in prison the night before his planned execution. Faith rests in adversity. Those who trust that God is at work in "all things" have the wonderful comfort that though the tapestry of life looks like nothing but a confusing mess, the day will come when it is turned over and His skillful handiwork will be clearly seen. Faith (trust) sees the certainty of that day.

BIRTH NAME: Marion Michael Morrison
DATE OF BIRTH: May 26, 1907
PLACE OF BIRTH: Winterset, Iowa
DATE OF DEATH: June 11, 1979
OCCUPATIONS: Actor, Director, Producer
CLAIM TO FAME: Leading role in 131 movies

JOHN WAYNE

About faith, John Wayne stated, "When the road looks rough ahead, remember the Man Upstairs and the word 'hope.' Hang onto both and tough it out."[132]

Shortly before his death, Wayne said, "I've always had deep faith that there is a Supreme Being; there has to be. To me that's just a normal thing to have that kind of faith. The fact that He's let me stick around a little longer, or She's let me stick around a little longer, certainly goes great with me—and I want to hang around as long as I'm healthy and not in anybody's way."[133]

BIRTH NAME: Kim Basinger
DATE OF BIRTH: December 8, 1953
PLACE OF BIRTH: Athens, Georgia
OCCUPATION: Actress
CLAIM TO FAME: *9½ Weeks* (1986)

KIM BASINGER

W hen asked what it is that keeps her "centered," Kim Basinger replied, "What keeps me centered? My faith in God, and my sense of humor."[134]

BIRTH NAME: Danny Labern Glover
DATE OF BIRTH: July 22, 1947
PLACE OF BIRTH: San Francisco, California
OCCUPATION: Actor
CLAIM TO FAME: *Iceman* (1984)

DANNY GLOVER

D anny Glover gave his thoughts on Mel Gibson's movie *The Passion of the Christ:* "When I saw the movie, I bore witness. I felt that I could be a better human being, that's what the movie is there to teach you."[135]

While the story of the brutal, suffering death of Jesus of Nazareth contains the most compelling example of forgiveness, to believe that its objective was to help us be better human beings is to entirely miss the point. The message of the cross isn't, "Here's an example of how you should live." It is, "You have failed to keep God's Law, and I am taking your punishment upon Myself—so you can have eternal life." It's too late for us to be "good" human beings.

The drink is already polluted. All of it must be poured out through repentance, and the glass refilled through the new birth.

BIRTH NAME: Richard Cavett
DATE OF BIRTH: November 19, 1936
PLACE OF BIRTH: Gibson, Nebraska
OCCUPATIONS: Comedian, Writer, Talk Show Host
CLAIM TO FAME: Host of the "Dick Cavett Show" (1969–1972)

DICK CAVETT

Dick Cavett mentioned in an interview that he finds it impossible to maintain any religious faith: "This is my religious problem: it would be wonderful to believe in the most fundamental way. It would make life easier, it would explain everything; it would give meaning where none is apparent; it would make tragedies bearable. If I went to a revival meeting, I have no doubt I could be one of the first to go down on his knees...

"It seems as if the only religion worth having is the simplest possible religion. But something about the fact that all it takes to make it so is deciding it *is* so puts me off. Knowing it could instantly make me much happier makes it somehow unworthy of having."[136]

The Christian faith *does* go against the grain in our performance-based world. We have to work hard at relationships, strive to get good grades in school, perform well on the job to be promoted, and so on. If we do well, we expect to be rewarded for our efforts. So it does seem illogical that something as important as our eternal destiny could be out of our hands.

In fact, this works-oriented principle applies in all other religions—followers must perform certain actions in order to be deemed worthy. With Christianity, on the other hand, God has done all the work. Through Christ's death on the cross, He has done all that is necessary for our salvation. The Bible tells us, "By grace you have been saved through faith, and that not of yourselves; it is the gift of God, not of works, lest anyone should boast."[137]

Man has apparently always felt he could do some good works to earn his salvation. When Jesus was asked, "What shall we do, that we may work the works of God?" He replied, "This is the work of God, that you believe in Him whom He sent."[138] Only our pride keeps us from accepting this simple truth.

BIRTH NAME: Carlos Ray Norris
DATE OF BIRTH: March 10, 1940
PLACE OF BIRTH: Ryan, Oklahoma
OCCUPATIONS: Martial Arts Instructor, Actor, Producer, Writer
CLAIM TO FAME: Professional World Middle-Weight Karate
Champion (1968–1974)

CHUCK NORRIS

When Chuck Norris was asked, "Are you a spiritual man —do you have God in your corner?" he answered, "Oh yes. I definitely feel I do have God in my corner. I've been very fortunate that way, I am very spiritual. I'm a very religious person. There's too many things in life for us to cope with without the faith of God. I think that's why there has been so many suicides today, the kids don't have the strength of God in their hearts and so they give up. As individuals they don't have the strength to cope. That's why the third leading cause of death for teenagers in America is suicide. That's very sad."[139]

BIRTH NAME: George Orson Welles
DATE OF BIRTH: May 6, 1915
PLACE OF BIRTH: Kenosha, Wisconsin
DATE OF DEATH: October 10, 1985
OCCUPATIONS: Actor, Director, Producer, Writer
CLAIM TO FAME: *Citizen Kane* (1941)

ORSON WELLES

After the success of his film *Citizen Kane*, Orson Welles announced that his next film would be about the life of Jesus Christ, and that he would play the lead role. However, he never made this film.[140] He later commented, "I have a great love and respect for religion, great love and respect for atheism. What I hate is agnosticism, people who do not choose."[141]

While it is virtuous to love and respect all men, I find it difficult to have respect for the *belief* of atheism. To anyone who examines the evidence, there can be no doubt that God exists. *Every* building has a builder. Everything made has a maker. The existence of the Creator is axiomatic (self-evident). The predictable question arises: "Then where did God come from?"

Professing atheists deny their God-given common sense, and often defend their beliefs by thinking that the question "Who made God?" can't be answered. They assume this gives them license to deny the existence of a Creator.

The question of who made God can be answered by simply looking at space and asking, "Does space have an end?" Obviously, it doesn't. If there is a brick wall with "The End" written on it, the question arises, "What's behind the brick wall?" Strain the mind though it may, we have to believe (have faith) that space has no beginning and no end.

The same applies with God. He has no beginning and no end. He is eternal. The Bible informs us that "time" is a dimension that God created, into which man has been subjected. It also tells us that one day time will no longer exist. That will be called "eternity." God Himself dwells outside of the dimension He created.[142] He dwells in eternity and is therefore not subject to time. He spoke history before it came into being. He can move through time as a man flips through a history book.

Humanity lives in the dimension of time; therefore logic and reason demand that everything *must* have a beginning and an end. But we can understand the concept of God's eternal nature the same way we understand the concept of space having no beginning and end—by faith. We simply *have* to believe these things are so, even though such thoughts put a strain on our distinctly insufficient cerebrum.

BIRTH NAME: Jerry Silberman
DATE OF BIRTH: June 11, 1933
PLACE OF BIRTH: Milwaukee, Wisconsin
OCCUPATIONS: Actor, Director, Writer, Producer
CLAIM TO FAME: *Young Frankenstein* (1974)

GENE WILDER

In answer to the question, "Do you have faith? Are you an optimist?" Gene Wilder answered, "Yes. I'm an optimist that—you're not talking about religion are you? Just…" The interviewer then clarified, "What do you believe in? Somebody out there, someplace?" Wilder said, "You asked Stephen Hawking this one. And he said, 'If by God you mean the mathematical equation that accounts for the creation of the solar systems and the black hole, yes, I do believe.' I'd give the same answer."[143]

BIRTH NAME: Raymond Joseph Teller
DATE OF BIRTH: February 14, 1948
PLACE OF BIRTH: Philadelphia, Pennsylvania
OCCUPATIONS: Entertainer/Magician, Artist, Writer
CLAIM TO FAME: PBS special "Penn & Teller Go Public" (1985)

TELLER

T eller said in reference to belief in God, "I have not the slightest need to believe in stuff that is not in some way verifiable. I believe in art, mind you. I don't believe that art is supernatural. I think that beauty and humor are wonderful things, and quite important to us—in fact, one of the major distinguishing features between us and some of the lesser species."[144]

He is right; the fact that we can appreciate art is one attribute that distinguishes us from the animals. Another distinguishing factor is that we can look at a painting and know that there was a painter. Art isn't "supernatural." It didn't paint itself.

BIRTH NAME: Alexander Rae Baldwin III
DATE OF BIRTH: April 3, 1958
PLACE OF BIRTH: Amityville, New York
OCCUPATIONS: Actor, Producer, Director, Writer
CLAIM TO FAME: *Beetlejuice* (1988)

ALEC BALDWIN

A lec Baldwin said, "I was 21 and asked myself, What am I doing? Why don't I go do something I want to do? Why don't I have faith in myself, God, life, the world?"[145]

In discussing a large earthquake that had shaken Los Angeles, he stated, "A lot of things broke. I wasn't scared but I was upset days later. I never had such a profound delayed reaction to something. The inevitability of it. It let a lot of people know there is a God. Los Angeles is a fairly godless place."[146]

BIRTH NAME: Katharine Houghton Hepburn
DATE OF BIRTH: November 8, 1907
PLACE OF BIRTH: Hartford, Connecticut
DATE OF DEATH: June 29, 2003
OCCUPATIONS: Actress, Writer
CLAIM TO FAME: *Morning Glory* (1933)

KATHARINE HEPBURN

Katharine Hepburn boldly asserted, "I'm an atheist, and that's it. I believe there's nothing we can know except that we should be kind to each other and do what we can for each other."[147]

It is much more reasonable to believe that this publication had no printer than to believe that there is no God. Nobody in his right mind could ever believe that the publication happened by chance —from nothing. There was no author, no paper, no ink, no cardboard, and no glue. The printed paper just came into being (from nothing), then trimmed itself into perfectly straight edges. All the words fell into place, forming coherent sentences, and then the graphics appeared. The pages fell into numerical order, and finally the book bound itself and slipped into a well-designed jacket. Wow. Anyone who could actually believe that has great faith.

The fact that there was a printer of this book is self-evident, so it would be intellectually insulting to even begin to argue for the case of the printer's existence. For the same reason, the Bible doesn't enter into the case for God's existence. It begins by simply declaring, "In the beginning God..."[148] and says, "The fool has said in his heart, 'There is no God.'"[149]

While it takes some skill to be an actor, intellect isn't necessary in order to be an atheist. Dwight Eisenhower said, "Any stupid person can deny the existence of a supernatural power because man's physical senses cannot detect it. But there cannot be ignored the influence of conscience, the respect we feel for the Moral Law, the mystery of first life... or the marvelous order in which the universe moves about us on this earth. All these evidence the handiwork of the beneficent Deity... That Deity is the God of the Bible and Jesus Christ, His Son."[150]

BIRTH NAME: Daniel Edward Aykroyd
DATE OF BIRTH: July 1, 1952
PLACE OF BIRTH: Ottawa, Ontario, Canada
OCCUPATIONS: Actor, Writer, Producer, Director
CLAIM TO FAME: "Saturday Night Live" (1975–1979)

DAN AYKROYD

Dan Aykroyd, who was an altar boy while he was growing up, stated, "I'm not what you would call a fervent practicing Catholic, but I do slip in the back door of church a couple times a year."

In response to a question about his faith in God, Aykroyd said, "I have a faith of a kind. I'm not a born-again Christian, but I have some faith. I think that God is in and around all of us, in everything and thus we're all connected. I have always believed that. I feel a link to the squirrels outside, and that's what God is to me. If He introduces Himself to me and sits me down and tells me something different, then I will reconsider my feelings."[151]

BIRTH NAME: Marlon Brando Jr.
DATE OF BIRTH: April 3, 1924
PLACE OF BIRTH: Omaha, Nebraska
OCCUPATIONS: Actor, Director, Producer
CLAIM TO FAME: *A Streetcar Named Desire* (1947)

MARLON BRANDO

Marlon Brando wrote in a letter, "I have been reading the Bible. It is full of beautiful thoughts but they don't mean much to me. Nana [Grandma], why do they tell you to fear God? I can't understand..."[152]

While experiencing a nervous breakdown, Brando wandered into a Christian Science reading room. He recalled, "I had never had much religion in my life—neither of my parents were believers—though a few times my mother had encouraged me to look for solace in the faith of my grandmother and Mary Baker Eddy. So I did, searching for anything that could help me understand what was wrong with me and make me feel better."[153]

Marlon Brando asked his grandmother an important question about why we should fear God. We should fear Almighty God because of who He is: He is the *Creator* of all things. Bear in mind that our greatest scientists cannot create (from nothing) even a tiny grain of sand. We can at best merely *recreate* using components that God has already made, but we cannot create something from nothing.

We can glimpse the greatness of the Creator by looking at His creation. Take one (very) small part of creation—the mind of man. The brain is a soft lump of tissue weighing about three pounds. It has four times as many nerve cells as there are people on Earth. With its 10 billion neurons, it can record 86 million bits of information each day of our lives. Supporting, protecting, and nourishing these 10 billion neurons are 100 billion glia cells, which make up half the mass of the brain.

I awoke recently in the middle of the night to words going around in my head. They were the words from a Beatles song that I had heard the previous afternoon. I had found a CD with Beatles tunes on it and as I listened each song brought back instantaneous recollections of different periods in my life—some triggered forty-year-old memories. All this automatic brain activity had nothing to do with my will. The human mind has a mind of it's own. It is complex, fantastic, incredible, wonderful—it's indescribable.

Then there's the other area of the brain that has complete independence—the conscience. It also has a mind of its own. It sits on a throne, like a self-regulating judge in the courtroom of the human mind, making moral judgments on activities of each day. If I am selfish or say something harshly, it will let me know. It will say, "That was a bit of a mean thing that you said. You had better apologize." If I am open to its reason, it causes my conscious mind to feel a sense of guilt.

Once again, these thoughts of guilt have nothing to do with my will. In fact, these accusations from my conscience may be *against* my will—I don't want to hear them, but they still come. This inner voice can be so strong that it drives many to drink, and some to suicide.

We take the incredible workings of the mind for granted, hardly giving them a second thought. Bear in mind that while you are reading the ink on this page, your mind is processing each ink marking to identify the letters. As you recognize the form of a word, its sound resonates in your mind and provides a word picture. You then make some sort of conclusion about each point, file the thought in your memory bank, and move on to the next statement. If music is playing in the background, perhaps in forty years when you hear the song again, your brain will instantly recall the words that you are reading at the moment... even if you don't want to.

If you believe that the human brain—an unspeakably remarkable miracle of brilliant technology—came about through some sort of cataclysmic accident, you are not using your God-given common sense. Your brain, and its capability to think logically and morally, came from your Creator.

The incredible complexity of creation and the vastness of the heavens speak of the awesome and fearful power of the Creator. Evolutionist Stephen Hawking wrote, "It would be very difficult to explain why the universe should have begun in just this way, except as the act of a God who intended to create beings like us." He also stated: "Then we shall...be able to take part in the discussion of the question of why it is that we and the universe exist. If we find the answer to that, it would be the ultimate triumph of human reason—for then we would know the mind of God."[154]

Those who understand that this creation is an expression of the Creator's unfathomable genius stand in awe of Him. They agree with the words of this hymn, "O Lord my God! When I in awesome wonder consider all the worlds Thy hands have made, I see the stars, I hear the rolling thunder, Thy power throughout the universe displayed."[155]

How can any thinking person not feel a measure of fear at a thunderclap so loud it shakes the earth, or a lightning flash that sends a bolt of electricity from one horizon to the other? Think of the power of a massive tornado or a gigantic tsunami, and the tender miracle of a butterfly emerging from a cocoon. The fear of God is the outcome of an understanding mind—that it is not "Mother Nature" that is displaying such power, but Almighty God.

Some people believe that we shouldn't fear God, but this thinking doesn't agree with Scripture. In fact, we are told that "the fear of the LORD is the beginning of wisdom."[156] Take a few moments to read the Psalms or the Book of Proverbs to see how the fear of God is enthusiastically applauded, because it is only right that we stand in awe of Him. Here is just one example of many:

Blessed is every one who fears the LORD, who walks in His ways. When you eat the labor of your hands, you shall be happy, and it shall be well with you. Your wife shall be like a fruitful vine in the very heart of your house, your children like olive plants all around your table. Behold, thus shall the man be blessed who fears the LORD.[157]

BIRTH NAME: Linda Evanstad
DATE OF BIRTH: November 18, 1942
PLACE OF BIRTH: Hartford, Connecticut
OCCUPATION: Actress
CLAIM TO FAME: "Dynasty" (1981–1989)

LINDA EVANS

When asked about how she coped with life's daily problems, Linda Evans said, "What I found for myself is that I was always looking outside to see whether things were working out all right. It was never Linda, you know? I did the impossible. I went up to the Pacific Northwest. I went into an ancient school of wisdom, and I spent years going inwards, meditating and, you know, finding God within me...

"I've completely found the peace that I was always looking for, either in a husband or friends or some kind of expression. I have personal peace, and that's what I suppose is working the best for me."[158]

Many people who are looking for peace have discovered that all the trappings of success cannot deal with the futility of life and the reality of death. Consider an Olympic gold-medallist high-diving champion who one night had insomnia. As he tossed and turned upon his bed, he began thinking deeply about the success he had attained and the gold medals he had won. To his dismay he realized that his success had not achieved what he had hoped. The excitement of winning, the photographers, the medals, and the fame had given him some sense of pleasure, but the fact that death was awaiting him left him with a complete sense of futility.

He rose from the bed and made his way to his diving pool. Because the moon was full, he didn't bother to turn the lights on. As he climbed the high diving board, he watched his shadow cast by the moonlight on the far wall. The routine had become so commonplace to him that he could confidently walk that board in the semi-darkness. At the end of the diving board, he prepared for the dive. He placed his feet together, and then pulled his arms up to a horizontal position. As he did so, his eyes caught a glimpse of his shadow on the far wall. All he could see was a perfect cross. His mind immediately raced back to something he learned in his Sunday school days: "But God demonstrates His own love toward us, in that while we were still sinners, Christ died for us." He suddenly felt unclean as he considered the Commandments he had broken. The sinless Son of God had come to pay the penalty for his sins. He whispered a verse he had memorized as a child: "For God so loved the world that He gave His only begotten Son, that whoever believes in Him should not perish but have everlasting life."

With tears in his eyes, the great athlete turned around, slowly made his way down to the bottom of the diving board, fell to his knees, and yielded his life to Jesus Christ. He was then able to go back to bed, and sleep peacefully.

In the morning he arose with a new sense of forgiveness of his sins. He made his way back to the pool, but to his utter astonishment, *it was completely empty*. The previous evening, the caretaker had emptied it and was just beginning the process of refilling.

Imagine if he had said, "It's true. I am a sinner. I believe that Jesus died for me. *Tomorrow* I will get right with God..." and taken that dive.

If you care about the eternal salvation of your soul, don't put it off until tomorrow. That may never come. Today, tell God that you are sorry for your sins, and then turn from them in humble repentance and place your trust in Christ.

BIRTH NAME: William Shatner
DATE OF BIRTH: March 22, 1931
PLACE OF BIRTH: Montreal, Quebec, Canada
OCCUPATIONS: Actor, Director, Writer, Producer
CLAIM TO FAME: Captain Kirk on "Star Trek" (1966–1969)

WILLIAM SHATNER

In answer to the question "Is there a God?" William Shatner replied, "There is, but we don't know where. Or who. And, indeed, why."[159]

I'm not sure for whom he is speaking when he says "we don't know." I suspect that it's on behalf of the human race, so I would like to take a moment to separate myself and millions of others from his statement. Possibly William Shatner doesn't know where God is, who He is, and why He is, so it would be more accurate for him to say, "*I* don't know."

God is omnipresent. His Name is Jehovah—the Great "I AM" —who revealed Himself to Moses through the burning bush on Mount Sinai, through the prophets, and then revealed Himself to humanity in the person of the Messiah, Jesus of Nazareth. He did this so that we could know Him and receive eternal life: "This is eternal life, that they may know You, the only true God, and Jesus Christ whom You have sent."[160]

BIRTH NAME: William Martin Joel
DATE OF BIRTH: May 9, 1949
PLACE OF BIRTH: Bronx, New York
OCCUPATIONS: Musician, Singer, Composer
CLAIM TO FAME: Single "Just the Way You Are" (1977)

BILLY JOEL

Billy Joel stated in an interview, "I still feel very much like an atheist in the religious aspects of things. But there are spiritual planes that I'm aware of that I don't know anything about and that I can't explain. That's why I think musicians are so revered and so important to our culture: We're the wizards, we sort of reveal a little bit of this extra-powerful communicative force. I recently rediscovered that I was enchanted with music and the creative arts as a little child because I thought there was an element of alchemy in them."[161]

BIRTH NAME: LaToya Yvonne Jackson
DATE OF BIRTH: May 29, 1956
PLACE OF BIRTH: Gary, Indiana
OCCUPATION: Recording Artist
CLAIM TO FAME: Member of the Jackson family

LATOYA JACKSON

Raised as a Jehovah's Witness, LaToya Jackson said, "I believe in a lot of the faith, but I am not a Jehovah Witness today. No. There are certain things I agree with and certain things I don't." Asked what she believed, Jackson answered, "I believe in

God. I'm very spiritual. I'm a spiritual person. I think being spiritual doesn't mean that you have to go to church every Sunday or throughout the week as long as you have that connection with God. And that's what I have and to me that's the most important thing that we speak."[162]

BIRTH NAME: Francis Albert Sinatra
DATE OF BIRTH: December 12, 1915
PLACE OF BIRTH: Hoboken, New Jersey
DATE OF DEATH: May 14, 1998
OCCUPATIONS: Actor, Singer, Producer, Composer, Director
CLAIM TO FAME: Known as the "King of the Bobbysoxers"

FRANK SINATRA

Frank Sinatra said of his beliefs, "I believe that God knows what each of us wants and needs. It's not necessary for us to make it to church on Sunday to reach Him. You can find Him anyplace. And if that sounds heretical, my source is pretty good: Matthew, Five to Seven, 'The Sermon on the Mount.'

"There are things about organized religion which I resent. Christ is revered as the Prince of Peace, but more blood has been shed in His name than any other figure in history. You show me one step forward in the name of religion, and I'll show you a hundred retrogressions...I'm for decency—period. I'm for anything and everything that bodes love and consideration for my fellow man. But when lip service to some mysterious deity permits bestiality on Wednesday and absolution[163] on Sunday—cash me out."[164]

We often formulate our opinions (right or wrong) about recording artists by what they sing. Frank Sinatra's famous song "My Way" (written by Paul Anka) begins with a reference to the end of this life—he was about to face "the final curtain." He lived a life that was full, having a few regrets, but then again, too few to mention. He planned his own course, and, what's more, he did it his way. When he had doubt, he ate it up and spat it out, stood tall and did it his way. The obvious is then stated. He says, "not in a shy way," that he did it his way. The final lyrics reveal what the song is really about: "To say the things he truly feels *and not the words of one who kneels*. The record shows I took the blows and did it *my way!*" (emphasis added).

It is normal for humans to rebel against the authority of God. We don't want "God" telling us what to do—"it's my life, I will do what I want." The Bible tells us, "[That is] because the mind of the flesh [with its carnal thoughts and purposes] is hostile to God, for it does not submit itself to God's Law; indeed it cannot" (Romans 8:7, Amplified Bible).

The problem with the "it's my life" philosophy is, it isn't my life at all. Everything I have is on loan from God, and one day I will give an account to Him.

BIRTH NAME: Maurice Joseph Micklewhite Jr.
DATE OF BIRTH: March 14, 1933
PLACE OF BIRTH: Bermondsey, England
OCCUPATIONS: Actor, Producer
CLAIM TO FAME: *Alfie* (1966)

MICHAEL CAINE

Michael Caine, in answering a question about his belief in God, said, "I see God as benign [kindly]. My own view is that I look around at everybody including the vicar and the priest, and the rabbi and the Muslim, and I suddenly realize they're human beings exactly like me...I threw them all out of the window at a very early age."[165]

I will never forget the film *Alfie*. Michael Caine played the role of a smooth-talking bachelor who committed adultery with a middle-aged married woman. It was a one-night fling. Unfortunately, she became pregnant and he encouraged her to have an abortion, rather than face the complexities of continuing the pregnancy.

He was present during the procedure, and out of curiosity he looked at the fetus. It was a *very* moving moment. He came out of the room looking pale and shocked, horrified that the fetus wasn't a blob of mucus, but was an actual baby. It was then that he realized he had been instrumental in taking the life of his own child.

The incident caused him to be very contemplative about life. The theme of the movie kicked in at that point: "What's it all about, Alfie?" While he was enjoying the pleasures of illicit sex, life was exciting. There wasn't too much to think about. But when Alfie considered the life he had just taken, when the reality of moral absolutes came into play, he was left soberly wondering about the purpose of his existence. Are humans just a species of animal, with no sense of right or wrong? Why then do we have the pangs of conscience when we take a life? If life has purpose, why does death snatch us from it? What is it all about?

It was that very thought that softened my heart to the gospel. I too asked the sobering question about life's purpose. Life had been good to me. At the age of 20 I had my own business, car, house, wife, and child. I owned a combined surf shop and custom leather jacket business. It was lucrative, and I had the freedom to slap a "Gone surfing" note on the door of my shop anytime I wanted. I couldn't have asked for more.

There was a problem, though. I realized that death could strike me or my loved ones at any moment. It was as though I had this big happiness bubble, and it was only a matter of time until the sharp pin of reality caused it to burst. Death made my existence futile. Happy though I was, I realized I was waiting around to die. So was every other human being. It made no sense.

Perhaps you have never had thoughts such as these. Maybe you're thinking, "Lighten up a little. Look on the positive side of things." Let me ask you a question: If someone were pushing you closer and closer toward a thousand-foot cliff, would you wonder why? I hope you would, and that you would see that it's in your immediate and best interest to get out of your predicament.

Every day, every hour, every minute, every second brings you closer to the inevitable cliff of death. Are you wondering why? Why is it that everything you hold dear to you will one day be ripped from your hands? How did you get into this situation, and how can you get out of it?

As I was researching for this book, I ran across a publication that listed every movie Hollywood ever made—every star, every director, screenwriter, etc. It was a huge volume, about the size of a phone book.

So many names I read were familiar. There's a sense of excitement when it comes to Hollywood celebrities; I'm sure you feel it. Just seeing their names in print sparks indelible memories from the silver screen. As I smiled at each recollection, I would very often see under their name the date of their death. It wasn't one or two who had passed on, but *thousands*.

I wondered how many of these shining stars faded into distant nobodies after they lost their youthful looks. How many became overnight has-beens, or destitute alcoholics or drug addicts who tried to escape from the painful reality that their glory days were over? I wondered how many had considered the question asked by Alfie, and then made peace with God before death snatched them into eternity.

Do you remember the thought-provoking words of George Lucas from the opening pages of this book? He considered the all-important question. He said, "Not having enough interest in the mysteries of life to ask the question, 'Is there a God or is there not a God?'—that is for me the worst thing that can happen. I think you should have an opinion about that. Or you should be saying, 'I'm looking. I'm very curious about this, and I am going to continue to look until I can find an answer, and if I can't find an answer, then I'll die trying.'"

BIRTH NAME: Myra Ellen Amos
DATE OF BIRTH: August 22, 1963
PLACE OF BIRTH: Newton, North Carolina
OCCUPATION: Recording Artist
CLAIM TO FAME: Album *Little Earthquakes* (1991)

TORI AMOS

Tori Amos said, "I'm just committed to uncovering the dark side of Christianity...Women have been sexually suppressed through the institution of Christianity...My relationship with the Christian God right now is very much about 'See you on Friday for margaritas'...He knows His gig but He doesn't know what it's like to be a red-headed girl in this body that has a lot of questions and not many answers."[166]

BIRTH NAME: Candace Helaine Cameron
DATE OF BIRTH: April 6, 1976
PLACE OF BIRTH: Panorama City, California
OCCUPATION: Actress
CLAIM TO FAME: "Full House" (1987)

CANDACE CAMERON-BURE

Candace Cameron-Bure was asked when she became a Christian and how it has affected her life and career. She said, "I thought I became a Christian when I was twelve, but realized I wasn't *really* one until I was about twenty-five. I had never turned from my sin. I didn't understand God's wrath and judgment. When that became clear to me, His grace and mercy then made sense.

"It affects my life and career tremendously in every aspect. Being a Christian is one of the hardest things in my life. I go against the grain every day, making choices that aren't easy in a world that promotes things I know are wrong. But God's Word—His truth— is more important to me than what others may think of me."[167]

BIRTH NAME: Walter Bruce Willis
DATE OF BIRTH: March 19, 1955
PLACE OF BIRTH: Idar-Oberstein, West Germany
OCCUPATIONS: Actor, Musician
CLAIM TO FAME: "Moonlighting" (1985–1989)

BRUCE WILLIS

Bruce Willis gave his thoughts on religion: "Organized religions in general, in my opinion, are dying forms. They were all very important when we didn't know why the sun moved, why weather changed, why hurricanes occurred, or volcanoes happened."[168]

According to Willis, "Modern religion is the end trail of modern mythology. But there are people who interpret the Bible literally. Literally! I choose not to believe that's the way. And that's what makes America cool, you know?"[169]

The popular actor brought up a good point. Why would anyone in his right mind believe the Bible, when it is full of stories that insult the intellect?

There are many reasons why I have no doubt it is the Word of God. Here is the main reason I believe it is the revelation of the Creator's will.

I was converted to Christianity in the early hours of April 25th, way back in 1972. I was dumbfounded at what happened to me that night. The change in my life was radical. However, my amazement didn't stop on the night when my eyes were suddenly opened to the reality of God. Over the following days the Scriptures actually told me about what I had experienced. It was like an instruction book that explained what would happen to an appliance after the power was switched on.

I felt like a completely new person. It was very strange. It wasn't simply a change of mind, or a change of lifestyle. The transformation was deep within my being. I was astounded that I had new desires. In my 22 years of life, I hadn't given God a serious thought for five seconds. Suddenly, it was all I thought about 24/7. Then I read this verse in the Bible: "If anyone is in Christ, he is a new creation; old things have passed away; behold, all things have become new."[170]

I was so different, it seemed as if I had been "born again." Then I read in Scripture about the new birth. I read that God was at work within me giving me the desire and the ability to do what pleased Him.[171] I would normally listen to music in my car, but instead I found myself turning the radio off because I had a peace I couldn't understand and an inexpressible joy. Then I read in Scripture of a peace that passes all understanding, and joy unspeakable. However, my salvation wasn't dependent upon newfound feelings or what I believed about the Bible, but on my relationship with the Savior. Salvation isn't a matter of *what* you know, but *who* you know.

I not only believe the Scriptures because they describe my conversion experience, I believe them because they address the problem of my sinful heart. They give me information on the origin of evil, my guilt, the necessity for a payment for sin, the provision for my forgiveness, and absolute assurance of everlasting life. No other "Holy Book" does this.

There are other reasons why I believe the Bible to be the revelation of the Creator's mind to humanity. The Scriptures contain hundreds of fulfilled prophecies, as well as many scientific and medical facts, written thousands of years before man discovered them. Here are some of them:[172]

1. Only in recent years has science discovered that everything we see is composed of invisible atoms. Scripture tells us that the "things which are seen were not made of things which do appear" (Hebrews 11:3).

2. Medical science has only recently discovered that blood-clotting in a newborn reaches its peak on the eighth day, then drops. The Bible consistently says that a baby must be circumcised on the eighth day.

3. At a time when it was believed that the earth sat on a large animal or a giant (1500 B.C.), the Bible spoke of the earth's free float in space: "He...hangs the earth upon nothing" (Job 26:7).

4. The prophet Isaiah also tells us that the earth is round: "It is he that sits upon the circle of the earth" (Isaiah 40:22). This is not a reference to a flat disk, as some skeptics maintain, but to a sphere. Secular man discovered this 2,400 years later. At a time when science believed that the earth was flat, it was the Scriptures that inspired Christopher Columbus to sail around the world.

5. God told Job in 1500 B.C.: "Can you send lightnings, that they may go, and say to you, Here we are?" (Job 38:35). The Bible here is making what appears to be a scientifically ludicrous statement—that light can be *sent*, and then manifest itself in speech. But did you know that radio waves travel at the speed of light? This is why you can have *instantaneous* wireless communication with someone on the other side of the earth. Science didn't discover this until 1864 when "British scientist James Clerk Maxwell suggested that electricity and light waves were two forms of the same thing" (*Modern Century Illustrated Encyclopedia*).

6. Science has discovered that stars emit radio waves, which are received on earth as a high pitch. God mentioned this in Job 38:7: "When the morning stars sang together..."

7. "Most cosmologists (scientists who study the structures and evolution of the universe) agree that the Genesis account of creation, in imagining an initial void, may be uncannily close to the truth" (*Time*, Dec. 1976).

8. Solomon described a "cycle" of air currents two thousand years before scientists "discovered" them. "The wind goes toward the south, and turns about unto the north; it whirls about continually, and the wind returns again according to his circuits" (Ecclesiastes 1:6).

9. Science expresses the universe in five terms: time, space, matter, power, and motion. Genesis 1:1,2 revealed such truths to the Hebrews in 1450 B.C.: "In the beginning [*time*] God created [*power*] the heaven [*space*] and the earth [*matter*]...And the Spirit of God moved [*motion*] upon the face of the waters." Thus, the first thing God tells man is that He controls all aspects of the universe.

10. The great biological truth concerning the importance of blood in our body's mechanism has been fully comprehended only in recent years. Up until 120 years ago, sick people were "bled," and many died because of the practice. If you lose your blood, you lose your life. Yet Leviticus 17:11, written 3,000 years ago, declared that blood is the source of life: "For the life of the flesh is in the blood."

11. *Encyclopedia Britannica* documents that in 1845, a young doctor in Vienna named Dr. Ignaz Semmelweis was horrified at the terrible death rate of women who gave birth in hospitals. As many as 30 percent died after giving birth. Semmelweis noted that doctors would examine the bodies of patients who died,

then, without washing their hands, go straight to the next ward and examine expectant mothers. This was their normal practice, because the presence of microscopic diseases was unknown. Semmelweis insisted that doctors wash their hands before examinations, and the death rate immediately dropped to a mere 2 percent.

Look at the specific instructions God gave His people for when they encounter disease: "And when he that has an issue is cleansed of his issue; then he shall number to himself seven days for his cleansing, and wash his clothes, and bathe his flesh in running water, and shall be clean" (Leviticus 15:13). Until recent years, doctors washed their hands in a bowl of water, leaving invisible germs on their hands. However, the Scriptures say specifically to wash hands under "running water."

12. "During the devastating Black Death of the fourteenth century, patients who were sick or dead were kept in the same rooms as the rest of the family. People often wondered why the disease was affecting so many people at one time. They attributed these epidemics to 'bad air' or 'evil spirits.' However, careful attention to the medical commands of God as revealed in Leviticus would have saved untold millions of lives. Arturo Castiglione wrote about the overwhelming importance of this biblical medical law: 'The laws against leprosy in Leviticus 13 may be regarded as the first model of sanitary legislation' (A History of Medicine)."[173]

With all these scientific facts revealed in ancient Scripture, how could any thinking person deny that the Bible is supernatural in origin? There is no other book in any of the world's religions (Vedas, Bhagavad-Gita, Koran, Book of Mormon, etc.) that contains scientific truth. In fact, they contain statements that are clearly unscientific.

I also mentioned that the Bible contains hundreds of prophecies that have been fulfilled to the smallest detail. For example, there are over 300 prophecies relating to Jesus' birth, ministry, death, and resurrection, each of which has been perfectly fulfilled. There are also numerous prophecies, commonly referred to as "signs of the times," that are yet to be fulfilled. They stand as evidence to show us that we are living in the days immediately preceding the Second Coming of Jesus Christ, when He comes "with power and great glory." Here they are for you to consider:[174]

There will be false Christs; wars and rumors of wars; nation rising against nation; famines; disease (pestilence); false prophets who will deceive many; and lawlessness (discarding of the Ten Commandments). The gospel will be preached in all the world. There will be earthquakes in various places; signs from heaven (in the sun, moon, and stars); and persecution against Christians in all nations. Men's hearts will fail them for fear of the future; they will be selfish, materialistic, arrogant, and proud. Homosexuality will increase; there will be blasphemy; cold-heartedness; overindulgence; brutality; rebellious youth; hatred of those who stand up for righteousness; ungodliness; pleasure-seeking; much hypocrisy. False Bible teachers will have many followers, be money-hungry, and slander the Christian faith.[175] Men will scoff and say that there was no such thing as the flood of Noah and that these "signs" have always been around. Their motivation for hating the truth will be their love of lust.[176]

The Scriptures tell us that these people make the big mistake of misunderstanding God. They don't recognize that God's time frame is not the same as ours. They think (in their willful ignorance) that His continued silence means that He doesn't see their sins. In truth, He is merely holding back His wrath, waiting for them to repent and escape the damnation of hell. Jesus warned that the sign to look for was the repossession of Jerusalem by the Jews. That happened in 1967, after 2,000 years, beginning the culmination of the signs of the times.

BIRTH NAME: Katherine Marie Ireland
DATE OF BIRTH: March 20, 1963
PLACE OF BIRTH: Glendale, California
OCCUPATIONS: Model, Actress, Author
CLAIM TO FAME: Supermodel turned actress

KATHY IRELAND

K athy Ireland said of her faith, "There was never a time in my life when I didn't believe in God. I didn't come to know Jesus as my Lord and Savior until I was 18 years old...I picked up the Bible and began to read...the Gospels. When I read about Jesus, I knew that I was reading the truth and my heart was convicted. I realized that I didn't know much about Him. What I came to understand was that He was a very cool guy. He not only became my Savior, but my best friend."[177]

She added, "My faith in God keeps me grounded. When I make God the priority in my life, everything else seems to fall into place."[178]

BIRTH NAME: George Timothy Clooney
DATE OF BIRTH: May 6, 1961
PLACE OF BIRTH: Lexington, Kentucky
OCCUPATIONS: Actor, Writer, Producer
CLAIM TO FAME: "ER" (1994–1999)

GEORGE CLOONEY

G eorge Clooney stated, "I don't believe in heaven and hell ...I don't know if I believe in God. All I know is that as an individual, I won't allow this life—the only thing I know to exist—to be wasted."[179]

Clooney described his ideal scenario for life: "The way you want to do it is like Cary Grant. Have a successful career, then...decide you're looking too old, leave the movies and never look back. Then at 80 years old have a stroke and drop dead. That's perfect."[180]

When I was 16 years old, a friend and I decided that after we turned 50 we would commit suicide. We thought life wasn't worth living when you were over the hill. I heard recently that my friend tragically committed suicide at the age of 54.

I have no plans to follow in his steps. I have discovered that, as I age, I gain a greater appreciation for life.

I don't think it's a perfect plan for a famous actor to have a stroke at the age of 80 and drop dead. I'm sure that no one in his right mind willingly gives up his life and those he loves. Fortunately, there is a better plan.

George Clooney said that he didn't believe in heaven and hell. It's amazing how many people think something doesn't exist because they don't believe in it. Let's say that I decide gravity is horrible. It injures and kills multitudes. Countless individuals die in plane crashes because of gravity. People fall off ladders; they tumble off mountains; they topple off roofs. They die while skydiving, bungee jumping, riding roller coasters, etc. This all happens because of the horrible law of gravity.

Tell me, if I become offended at the results of gravity, or if I don't believe it exists, is it going to change the reality of its existence? Of course not. The law of gravitational pull isn't changed in the slightest, just because I don't like it and choose not to believe in it. Besides, if it weren't for gravity, we would all be dead and our lifeless bodies would be spinning through space. Gravity is good, not bad. It is there to preserve, not to destroy. It is only those who transgress its precepts who suffer.

The same applies with the Moral Law (the Ten Commandments). How can we say that a law that forbids murder, adultery, theft, and lying is bad? Only those who transgress its precepts will suffer, and the Bible warns that hell is the full and final result of transgression.

A legitimate question arises: Could the Bible be wrong about hell? Remember, the source of the claim isn't the word of fallible man; it is the Word of an infallible Creator. But let's infer for a moment that there is no Judgment Day and therefore no hell. That would mean that the Scriptures are a huge hoax, in which more than forty authors collaborated (over a period of 3,000 years) to produce a document revealing God's character as "just." They portrayed Him as an impartial Judge, who warned that He would eventually punish murderers, rapists, liars, thieves, adulterers, etc. Each of those writers (who professed to be religious) therefore bore false witness, transgressing the very Commandments they claimed to be true. It would mean that Jesus Christ was a liar, and that all the claims He made about the reality of the coming Judgment were therefore false. It would also mean that He gave His life in vain, as did multitudes of martyrs who down through the ages have given their lives for their belief in Christ.

Also keep in mind something we have already looked at: if there is no ultimate justice, then the Creator of all things is unjust. He sees the murder and rape of multitudes and couldn't care less, making Him worse than a corrupt human judge who refuses to bring criminals to justice.

Here's the good news if there is no hell: You won't know a thing after you die. It will be the end. No heaven, no hell. Just nothing. Sadly, you won't even know that it's good news.

Here's the bad news if the Bible is right and there is eternal justice: You will find yourself standing before the judgment throne of a holy and perfect Creator who has seen your thought-life and every secret sin you have ever committed. Nothing has been hidden from the eyes of God. You and I have a multitude of sins, and God must by nature carry out justice. Ask Him to remind you of the sins of your youth. Ask Him to bring to remembrance your secret sexual sins, the lies, the gossip, and other idle words. You may have forgotten your past, but God hasn't.

The Bible continually claims that there will be a great and terrible Day of the Lord. If we don't believe it, it is still true. It will still happen. Yet, there is good news—incredibly good news. We deserve judgment, but God offers us mercy. Through the cross of Jesus Christ, He paid our fine so that we could leave the courtroom. He destroyed the power of death for all who obey Him. Jesus promised that if you obey Him, you will know the truth, and the truth will make you free.[181] Please, don't wait any longer. Think of the Commandments you have broken. Think of what He suffered on the cross on your behalf. Then confess your sins and turn from them. Tell God you are truly sorry, then trust the Savior as you would trust yourself to a parachute. The moment you do that, you will pass from death into life. You will be transformed by God Himself. If you are not sure how to do this, see Psalm 51 at the back of this book.

BIRTH NAME: Delloreese Patricia Early
DATE OF BIRTH: July 6, 1931
PLACE OF BIRTH: Detroit, Michigan
OCCUPATIONS: Actress, Musician
CLAIM TO FAME: "Touched by an Angel" (1994–2003)

DELLA REESE

When asked about her background, Della Reese explained that her faith was rooted in her childhood: "In my house, God was part of the family. It wasn't a thing we did on Sunday. It's bred in me. The show is just affirmation for me that God has given me a place to teach what I know."[182]

An ordained minister, Reese believes, "If you're in a twister, in a tornado, God is in there too, and he loves you. Whatever you're going through at this moment, God is in there. And being all the power, you can get some help here, and people need to know that." Asked if she had ever been at a point her life when she lost faith, Reese replied, "Not my faith...I have been without money, but I've never been without my faith."[183]

BIRTH NAME: Phyllis Ada Driver
DATE OF BIRTH: July 17, 1917
PLACE OF BIRTH: Lima, Ohio
OCCUPATIONS: Actress, Comedian
CLAIM TO FAME: One of the first female stand-up comics

PHYLLIS DILLER

In speaking of what she thinks will happen in the year 3000, Phyllis Diller said, "The constants all through the centuries will be the same; wine, women and song...We were not created by a deity. We created the deity in our image...

"Life began on this planet when the first amoeba split. Mankind will still be seeking God, not accepting that God is a spirit; can't see it, touch it, only feel it. It's called LOVE."[184]

Phyllis Diller is right. God is a Spirit. We are also told that He is immortal and He is invisible. She is also right about Him being "love."

Here's a thought for those who have trouble with believing in something that is invisible. The wind is invisible. We can't see it. No one has ever seen it. We can, however, see the *effects* of the wind, such as smoke blowing or a flag waving. Television waves are invisible. We can't see them, but they surround us. We can pick up those invisible waves and see them through a receiver called a television set.

There are those who think there is no such thing as the "soul." They believe we are simply a body, nothing else. Then consider a surfer who is viciously attacked by a dozen hungry sharks. They assault him in shallow water and rip off his legs and his arms. Paramedics rescue what is left of him, and miraculously he lives.

He is physically only half the man he was, but he is still a complete person. The sharks didn't swim off with half of his soul. He still retains his character, his personality—he is still a complete self.

The plumb line of the Bible says that we are more than body and soul. We are body, soul, and spirit. The body is the house in which we live. The soul is the area of our emotions, our will, and our conscience—the "*self*-conscious" part of us. But our spirit is our *God*-conscious part. We are told in Scripture that the spirit is dead because of sin. We are not conscious of God; the "receiver" is switched off. We know that He exists, but we are not aware of His immediate and continual presence—until our spirit is made alive when we are born again—"born of the Spirit."

I am not saying these things because they are something I *believe*. I *know* these things to be true because I was once spiritually dead. I had as much awareness of spiritual things as a dead man has of physical things. I look back at my "B.C." (Before Conversion) days and see a different person. I see a youth who rarely thought about God. I never had to. The only real tragedy that ever stopped me for a moment was the loss of my beloved dog. It ran across a road in front of me and was hit by a car and killed. That night I thought about God.

Other than rattling off the Lord's prayer habitually each night in about ten seconds, I hardly gave God a second thought.

However, I can say that since my conversion in 1972 (God is my witness), I have been *consumed* with thoughts of Him. He is my life. I have a wonderful wife whom I deeply love. But I love God more. My affection for Sue didn't decrease after I was converted, it's just that she is the gift and God is the Giver. No one should ever love a gift more than the giver.

BIRTH NAME: Pamela Denise Anderson
DATE OF BIRTH: July 1, 1967
PLACE OF BIRTH: Ladysmith, British Columbia
OCCUPATION: Actress
CLAIM TO FAME: "Baywatch" (1992–1997)

PAMELA ANDERSON

During an interview with Pamela Anderson, a caller asked, "You seem really grounded. I wanted to know if you had— what your religious beliefs were, or spiritual beliefs were?" Anderson answered, "Well, I believe in God. I definitely believe that He is the reason that I've gotten through everything that I have. And I go to church. My kids go to Sunday school. And it's definitely a part of my life." Asked by the interviewer if that was the Protestant faith, she replied, "No, non-denominational. Just I believe in God."[185]

BIRTH NAME: Maureen FitzSimons
DATE OF BIRTH: August 17, 1920
PLACE OF BIRTH: Dublin, Ireland
OCCUPATION: Actress
CLAIM TO FAME: *Jamaica Inn* (1939)

MAUREEN O'HARA

An interviewer commented to Maureen O'Hara that many of her contemporaries have died. "Yes," she replied. "I hate to tell you, most of them have. Almost all of my friends in the picture business have died." In discussing how much to say about them in a book she's writing, she said, "Well, do you know what I'm afraid of? I'm getting on a little bit in years, as you know. And I'm terrified about the day that I enter the gates of heaven and God says to me, 'Just a minute. Where did you get permission to tell that story?' What am I going to say to God?"[186]

The question was asked, "And you believe there is a God..." to which she responded, "Oh, I sure do. How could you have had such a wonderful life as me if there wasn't a God directing?"[187]

BIRTH NAME: Phillip Calvin McGraw
DATE OF BIRTH: September 1, 1950
PLACE OF BIRTH: Vinita, Oklahoma
OCCUPATIONS: Psychologist, TV Talk Show Host
CLAIM TO FAME: TV Psychologist on "Oprah!"

DR. PHIL MCGRAW

Dr. Phil was asked, "Is the religious person better off, just by the nature of the fact that they have faith?" He replied, "I think life without faith would be pretty scary. You know, I'm kind of a chicken. And I remember when I was young, I got baptized at a very young age. And I wasn't sure whether or not I believed it, but my thinking was, cover your bets, boy, because if, in fact, there is an afterlife, then you want to be on the winning team." Asked if he believed there was an afterlife, he stated, "Absolutely, without a doubt."[188]

He was later asked if having faith runs "in the face of logic." Dr. Phil answered, "The truth is, there are so many things in our life that we don't have empirical proof of, that we don't understand. You know, I don't understand electricity, but it comes in real handy. I don't understand everything there is about faith and about the spiritual world, but I tell you what, there are so many questions I can't answer without it, that it feels awfully right to me."[189]

BIRTH NAME: Michael Moore II
DATE OF BIRTH: April 23, 1954
PLACE OF BIRTH: Flint, Michigan
OCCUPATIONS: Documentarian, Director, Producer, Actor, Writer
CLAIM TO FAME: Documentary "Roger and Me" (1989)

MICHAEL MOORE

A sked if he believed there was a God, Michael Moore answered, "Yes, there is. I don't know how you define that, but yeah. I'm a Catholic, I believe in God. I don't believe in a lot of what the Catholic Church believes in, but..."[190]

BIRTH NAME: Albert William Upton
DATE OF BIRTH: July 15, 1960
PLACE OF BIRTH: Los Angeles, California
OCCUPATIONS: Actor, Writer
CLAIM TO FAME: "Eight is Enough" (1977–1981)

WILLIE AAMES

W illie Aames shared how he came to his faith: "I went through the 12-step program, and I don't mean to disparage 12-step programs, because they're good and people who need it should do them. But I'm sitting there, and they're talking about needing to get in touch with 'God as you understand it.' I'm sitting there thinking, 'I'm an alcoholic idiot nitwit jerk. If I'm going to follow a god, why would I want to follow a god of my creation? That would be an alcoholic idiot nitwit jerk god.'

"The girl I was dating at the time heard this preacher on the radio, and she thought his message was something I should hear. I thought, 'Great; a preacher. Just what I need,' but she really encouraged me to check him out. We did, and then we checked out his church. Many of the people there had experienced ruined marriages and divorce, as I had, but they offered me hope, and I remember thinking, 'That's what I need.' And that hope was in Jesus Christ."[191]

Aames continued, "Strength doesn't come from what goes on around you. It comes from what's inside you, and that comes from Jesus Christ...I tell kids that people will let them down and people will hurt them. But Jesus Christ will never let them down and never hurt them."[192]

BIRTH NAME: Marvin Neil Simon
DATE OF BIRTH: July 4, 1927
PLACE OF BIRTH: Bronx, New York
OCCUPATIONS: Writer, Producer
CLAIM TO FAME: One of Broadway's most successful playwrights

NEIL SIMON

In reminiscing about his youth, Neil Simon said, "You did not boast about your good fortune because God would certainly punish a boaster. I was not overly religious, in fact hardly religious at all, but your culture, by osmosis, or what you hear around the dinner table as a boy, brands fears and superstitions into your mind forever."[193]

BIRTH NAME: Joseph Levitch
DATE OF BIRTH: March 16, 1926
PLACE OF BIRTH: Newark, New Jersey
OCCUPATIONS: Comedian, Actor, Writer
CLAIM TO FAME: Comedy Duo with Dean Martin

JERRY LEWIS

The following random excerpts are taken from an interview with Larry King:

LEWIS: "We don't need a wind screen on that God-damn mic."

LEWIS: "Thank God."

LEWIS: "And they said, 'Oh, God, you're sure?'"

LEWIS: "God, yes. I'm here."

LEWIS: "Oh, God, yes."

LEWIS: "Oh, God, yes. Oh, God."

LEWIS: "Oh, God, yes..."

LEWIS: "No. Oh, God, no."

In reference to a moment when he was reunited with Dean Martin (after twenty years) in front of a live audience, Jerry Lewis said, "I prayed to God that moment that He would give me one thing to say. I prayed on his [Dean's] whole walk toward me, 'What am I going to say?' And when he put his arm around me and then pulled away, I said, 'You working?' Thank God it came. The laugh was there. And we went on."

LEWIS: "Oh, my God."

LEWIS: "Oh, God, yes."

LEWIS: "Oh, God, yes."

LEWIS: "Oh, God, yes."

LEWIS: "Oh, God, does he know what he's talking about."

LEWIS: "Oh, God, yes."

LEWIS: "Oh, God, I love that."

KING: "Thank God for you, Jerry."[194]

Sadly, the use of God's name without due reverence or in place of a filth word has become a common part of contemporary speech. While researching hundreds of celebrity interviews, I found that "God" was mentioned numerous times in blasphemy. Yet, the interview with the likeable Lewis was thoroughly flavored with "Thank God," "God knows," and "God bless you." It seems that their concept of "God" isn't the same as the one who revealed Himself through the Bible. It warns, "The LORD will not hold him guiltless who takes His name in vain."[195]

BIRTH NAME: Carrie Frances Fisher
DATE OF BIRTH: October 21, 1956
PLACE OF BIRTH: Los Angeles, California
OCCUPATIONS: Actress, Writer
CLAIM TO FAME: Princess Leia in *Star Wars* (1977)

CARRIE FISHER

Carrie Fisher admitted, "I love the idea of God, but it's not stylistically in keeping with the way I function. I would describe myself as an enthusiastic agnostic who would be happy to be shown that there is a God.[196] I can see that people who believe in God are happier. My brother is. My dad is, too. But I doubt."[197]

It may be true that those members of her family who are Christians are happier, but that's not always the case. I didn't become a Christian because I saw that Christians were happier than I was. I became a Christian because I realized that I had sinned against God. Happiness had nothing to do with it. The moment I understood that God saw lust as adultery, and that He was going to have a Day of Judgment, I knew I was in big trouble. It was then that Jesus' death on the cross began to make sense to me.

Not long after my conversion I went into a deep depression—something I had never experienced in my happy-go-lucky B.C. days. It didn't make me doubt my faith for a moment; in fact, it actually strengthened it. Storms make the roots go deeper. This lesson in the natural realm also applies in the spiritual.

If my motive for becoming a Christian had been one of seeking happiness, I would have been disillusioned by that terrible experience, and I may have turned my back on God. Those who come to Christ because of a promise of true peace, happiness, joy, or a better life often fall away when trials come.[198]

BIRTH NAME: Andrew Rooney
DATE OF BIRTH: January 14, 1919
PLACE OF BIRTH: Albany, New York
OCCUPATION: Reporter
CLAIM TO FAME: Commentator on "60 Minutes" (1978–present)

ANDY ROONEY

When asked, "Do you believe in God?" Andy Rooney responded, "No, of course I don't, and anyone who tells you that there is a God who makes His or Her presence known to him or her is hallucinating or not telling the truth."[199]

To claim authoritatively that there is no God, or that someone who says there is a God is lying, is to make what is commonly called an "absolute" statement. For me to make an absolute statement (and for it to be true), I must have absolute knowledge. Let me give you an example.

If I say, "There is no gold in China," for that statement to be true, I need to *know* that there is no gold in China. I need to have absolute knowledge. I must know what's in every riverbed, in every rock, in all the soil, and in every mouth, because if there is even one gold filling in one Chinese tooth, my statement is false. To make an absolute statement, I need absolute knowledge. Conversely, to say, "There *is* gold in China," I don't need absolute knowledge. All I need is for a Chinese gentleman to yawn, and the moment I spot a gold filling, I can say with certainty that gold exists in China.

So anyone who has come to know God by trusting in Jesus Christ is qualified to state truthfully that God does exist. But unless Andy Rooney has absolute knowledge, he cannot honestly claim that there is no God. The only one qualified to make such a state-ment (the only one who has absolute knowledge) is God Himself —and I don't think Andy Rooney would claim to be God.

For years I enjoyed Andy Rooney's tongue-in-cheek comments about life, probably because I could so often identify with his point of view. For instance, I caught my wife being violent the other night. We went to bed early so that we could read books. I lasted my usual three minutes before feeling sleepy, so I closed the book, turned my bedside lamp off, and shut my eyes.

A couple of minutes later, I was awakened by a thunderous noise. I must have been in that almost-asleep sensitive mode when Sue violently turned the page of her book. The sound was deafen-ing. I opened my eyes and said, "Do you have to turn the pages over so *violently?*" She didn't know what I was talking about, so I took hold of the book to show her what she was doing. But when I turned its page, the dumb thing hardly made any noise at all. I gave it back to her and heard her mumbling something about me being weird. I closed my eyes and drifted off.

Minutes later, during the almost-asleep sensitive stage, our dog barked. It decided that the best place to bark was by our bedroom door. It barked and barked. As far as I could tell it was the same bark, thirty times. What word was it saying over and over, and why does it need to say it thirty times to get the point across? I thought some mean thoughts, then drifted off to sleep.

It was during that almost-asleep sensitive stage that the phone rang. It was right beside my bed, so I picked it up and wondered why my son-in-law had such a small-sounding voice. It was when I pulled the phone back to see what was wrong with it that I realized I was talking into the earpiece. I turned it around to hear, "Were you asleep?" I said I was, but that it was okay he called. I don't know why I said that, because it was really insensitive for him to call at the late hour of 8:05 p.m. He was apologetic, so I consoled him, hung up the phone and drifted back to sleep.

Moments later, during that almost-asleep sensitive stage, I heard a loud *beep-beep-beep-beep*. Some bright spark had put the phone on the cradle backwards. I could hear Sue laughing about something. Perhaps she is right: I am a bit weird.

For the last twenty years I have been getting up most nights to pray, read the Bible, and write. She often hears me bump into things as I walk around in the dark. That's a little weird. Or now and then she hears the clank of a spoon on a cereal bowl at 2:00 a.m. I also ride a kid's bike to and from work. The small bike is light, so it fits into the back of our van if I don't want to ride home some days. I do eat cereal three times a day. That's weird. My son-in-law often stares at me while I'm eating, saying, "I don't believe it. Cereal. Every day. Weird." Of course I also eat vegetables most days, but cereal is quick and easy and it helps me to maintain my weight. Besides, I like it.

I also run everywhere. Sue told me that it didn't look good, when I once ran out of a bank. Our ministry has two locations and most days I run the hundred yards between the two. I run because it's quick. I also run because I hate walking. I hate running, but I hate walking more. A businessman said that he admires me because he often sees a blur go past his office window. That's me, running. He doesn't see what my staff see. After also running up the flight of stairs, I have to lie on the floor to get my breath back. Is that weird or what?

Perhaps we are all a little strange. You probably don't think you are weird because you have sane reasons for doing what you do, whether it be mumbling to yourself on occasion, yelling at politicians on TV, or tossing and turning to get into your favorite sleeping position before you doze off.

But we often do these seemingly weird things because God has given us instincts. For example, turning over in bed a few times doesn't just happen before we go to sleep. It happens all night. One reason is so that the body's blood flow isn't hindered for too long. If the blood isn't able to circulate throughout the body, we would develop bed sores and perhaps gangrene.

So next time you see a blur go past your window, or see a grown man on a kid's bike, or hear a dog saying the same word over and over, withhold any thoughts of weirdness. There may be a reasonable explanation.

BIRTH NAME: Barbara Jean Moorehead
DATE OF BIRTH: August 23, 1934
PLACE OF BIRTH: Tucson, Arizona
OCCUPATION: Actress
CLAIM TO FAME: "I Dream of Jeannie" (1965–1970)

BARBARA EDEN

Barbara Eden was interviewed a year after her only child died of a heroin overdose. A caller inquired, "Do you have a routine where you read the Bible each day, or how are you dealing with this loss?" Barbara Eden said, "Well, you know, I had a thought today, actually, when I was thinking about the miners down in the coal mine and how awful it was not only for them, but for their loved ones up on top, and how many of us in the world have to deal with tragedy. And I think the only way we can deal with it is—I happen to have a faith in God, of a higher power, whatever you want to call it.

"I think we're put on this earth for a reason and it is to be productive...You know, life is a gift."[200]

She continued, "Did my faith ever waver or does it ever waver? No. No, it doesn't because I look at whatever you want to call it as a more impersonal creative force in the world. I don't think it's out to do good for us or to do bad for us. I think it's up to us."[201]

BIRTH NAME: Allen Stewart Konigsberg
DATE OF BIRTH: December 1, 1935
PLACE OF BIRTH: Brooklyn, New York
OCCUPATIONS: Actor, Director, Writer, Musician, Comedian
CLAIM TO FAME: *Annie Hall* (1977)

WOODY ALLEN

Woody Allen told an interviewer, "I do occasionally envy the person who is religious naturally, without being brainwashed into it or suckered into it by all the organized hustlers. It would just never occur to such a person for a second that the world isn't about something."[202]

Don't let the many "organized hustlers" keep you from getting right with God. I am deeply offended and embarrassed by money-hungry preachers, and I'm sure I wouldn't be the only one to rejoice if someone made a whip and cleared the temple of modern moneychangers.

Allen also said of the afterlife, "The chief problem about death, incidentally, is the fear that there may be no afterlife—a depressing thought, particularly for those who have bothered to shave. Also, there is the fear that there is an afterlife but no one will know where it's being held."[203]

BIRTH NAME: Larry Flynt
DATE OF BIRTH: November 1, 1942
PLACE OF BIRTH: Lakeville, Kentucky
OCCUPATIONS: Publisher, Actor, Producer
CLAIM TO FAME: Publisher of *Hustler* magazine

LARRY FLYNT

L arry Flynt bluntly confessed, "I have left my religious conversion behind[204] and settled into a comfortable state of atheism. I have come to think that religion has caused more harm than any other idea since the beginning of time."[205]

It is true that man has used religion for political and financial gain. It has done irreparable damage throughout history. Nazi Germany had "God With Us" engraved in German on the belts of Nazi soldiers."

The use of God for personal gain still occurs today. You can become a "reverend" for a few dollars through the tabloid classifieds and then further your agenda with the world's blessing, no matter how much it smears the name of Christ. This is nothing new. The atrocities committed by the Roman Catholic church in the name of Christianity during "the Crusades" have brought great disrepute to the gospel. Other mainline Protestant (non-Catholic) churches have used Christianity to further godless agendas.

Jesus said that there will be some who, in their error, cause mayhem and murder in the name of God. He warned, "The time is coming that whoever kills you will think that he offers God service." However, He informs us that these are not true believers: "And these things they will do to you because they have not known the Father nor me."[206]

Jesus instructed His followers to love their enemies. We are to do good to those who spitefully use us. So if a man puts a knife into someone's back in the name of Christianity, you may conclude that something isn't quite right.

If we human beings can detect hypocrisy, how much more will God? He will deal with it on Judgment Day. So it's important that we ourselves are free from hypocrisy, and that our motives are always pure. Abraham Lincoln rightly surmised, "I know that the Lord is always on the side of right. But it is my constant anxiety and prayer that I—and this nation—should be on the Lord's side."

BIRTH NAME: Jacqueline Joyner
DATE OF BIRTH: March 3, 1962
PLACE OF BIRTH: St. Louis, Illinois
OCCUPATION: Track & Field Athlete
CLAIM TO FAME: Olympic champion; considered one of the greatest athletes of all time

JACKIE JOYNER-KERSEE

Jackie Joyner-Kersee spoke of the role faith played in her childhood: "It was clear Jesus was the guiding force of our family life. On Sunday we went to church and Sunday school, no questions asked. And we looked forward to it...I accepted Christ as a young child as a result." [207]

About her mother's death at a young age, Jackie said, "It brought home what Mom had always told me—that the next day or even the next second isn't promised to us. She'd shared with me how important it is to keep in mind my goals and my eternal future with God." [208]

As for what keeps her grounded with her success, she said, "God is the one who gave me my success—and He can take it away if I don't handle it well. Knowing where my true success and self-worth come from puts my life in the right perspective."[209]

BIRTH NAME: Liza May Minnelli
DATE OF BIRTH: March 12, 1946
PLACE OF BIRTH: Los Angeles, California
OCCUPATION: Actress
CLAIM TO FAME: *Cabaret* (1972)

LIZA MINNELLI

When asked during an interview, "What is [your] secret on looking so fantastic?" Liza Minnelli said, "I think it—I think it's my faith. My faith in God and in God through people and I believe that mother Mary watches over me as well as my own mom."[210]

BIRTH NAME: Elizabeth Rosemond Taylor
DATE OF BIRTH: February 27, 1932
PLACE OF BIRTH: London, England
OCCUPATION: Actress
CLAIM TO FAME: *National Velvet* (1944)

ELIZABETH TAYLOR

After several brushes with death due to health problems, Elizabeth Taylor was asked, "Do you think... there's a cloud hanging over you?" She responded, "No, I don't, because I'm still here... Each time that I have almost died, while I have been recuperating and not quite knowing whether I was going to make it or not, you have time, plenty of time. Even an hour is plenty of time when you don't know whether you are going to live or not. And you think: Why did I make it? Why am I not dead? Everything indicated that I should be. There must be some reason that God wants me to live. There must be something left for me to do. And I have to find out what that something is and go out there and do it!"[211]

BIRTH NAME: Christopher Reeve
DATE OF BIRTH: September 25, 1952
PLACE OF BIRTH: New York City, New York
OCCUPATIONS: Actor, Author, Producer, Director
CLAIM TO FAME: *Superman* (1978)

CHRISTOPHER REEVE

When asked about his faith in God, Christopher Reeve said, "Well, believe it or not, in my book, *Nothing is Impossible*, I have divided it into two chapters: the search for spirituality, one chapter is on faith. The other chapter is on religion. In a way they're kind of different for me. Because as a kid, religion seemed to be a bit scary, that somebody sort of—you were kind of guilty while going into church. And it sort of sometimes made you feel bad. But over time, you know, I have actually become a Unitarian. And we embrace that because it's all inclusive and it's about the goodness in people. That God, you know, loves us and that he assumes that we are good. And also it just assumes that we have a moral compass inside us. And we kind of know what's right."[212]

In an online chat, Reeve was asked about something he wrote in his book *Still Me:* "Your spirit leaves your body at one point and looks down on it from the corner of the hospital room. Do you draw any spiritual conclusion from that?" He replied, "I feel strongly that we are not our bodies. In fact, if a person says 'my body,' who is the 'me' that is being referred to? Clearly, the spirit and body are two different things. And beyond that, I'm still searching for the meaning of it all."[213]

BIRTH NAME: Alicia Christian Foster
DATE OF BIRTH: November 19, 1962
PLACE OF BIRTH: Los Angeles, California
OCCUPATIONS: Actress, Director, Producer
CLAIM TO FAME: *Taxi Driver* (1976)

JODIE FOSTER

Jodie Foster said about God, "I absolutely believe...that there is no direct evidence, so how could you ask me to believe in God when there's absolutely no evidence that I can see? I do believe in the beauty and the awe-inspiring mystery of the science that's out there that we haven't discovered yet, that there are scientific explanations for phenomena that we call mystical because we don't know any better."[214]

Secular scientists would have us believe that there is no evidence for a Creator, claiming that there is a mass of evidence for a godless evolution. But if every creature "evolved" with no Creator's involvement, there are numerous problems. Take for instance the first bird. Was it a male or a female? Let's say it was a male. How did it produce offspring without a mate? If a female evolved, why did it evolve with differing, but complementary, reproductive organs? Did it evolve by chance, or did it evolve because it knew it was needed by the male of the species? Why was it needed if the male survived on its own? How did it know what needed to be evolved, and how to evolve it? Did the first bird breathe? Did it breathe before it evolved lungs? How did it do this? Why did it evolve lungs if it was happily surviving without them?

Did the bird have a mouth? How did it eat before it evolved a mouth? How did the bird have energy if it didn't eat (because it didn't yet have a mouth)? Where did the mouth send the food before a stomach evolved? How did the bird see what there was to eat before its eyes evolved? Apply these same thoughts to all the other creatures on this earth that some people would have us believe evolved.

There are also those who think everything began with a Big Bang. But try to think of any explosion that has produced order. Does a terrorist bomb create harmony? Big bangs cause chaos. How could a big bang produce a rose, apple trees, fish, sunsets, the seasons, hummingbirds, polar bears, dogs, cats, lions, tigers and elephants—thousands of birds and animals, each with its own eyes, nose, and mouth? Think about that for a moment.

It seems strange that scientists who believe we were brought into being by a godless big bang would remark about "grand design" in the universe. How can there be any design without a designer? Design speaks of order. No explosion produces design.

Consider these quotes from secular sources:

> According to *U.S. News & World Report* (March 31, 1997), "New scientific revelations about supernovas, black holes, quarks, and the big bang even suggest to some scientists that there is a 'grand design' in the universe."

> Jim Holt, science writer for the *Wall Street Journal*, wrote, "The universe suddenly exploded into being... The big bang bears an uncanny resemblance to the Genesis command."

Try this interesting experiment: Empty your garage of every piece of metal, wood, paint, rubber, and plastic. *Make sure there is nothing there.* Nothing. Then wait for ten years and see if a Mercedes evolves. Try it. If it doesn't appear, leave it for 20 years. If that doesn't work, try it for 100 years. Then try leaving it for 10,000 years.

Here's what will produce the necessary blind faith to make the evolutionary process believable: leave it for 250 million years. For many people, vast amounts of time makes the utterly impossible seem possible.

Evolution is intellectual suicide. It is an embarrassment, and I'm embarrassed to admit I once had faith that it was true. Respected scientist Professor Louis Bounoure (Director of Research, National Center of Scientific Research) said, "Evolution is a fairy tale for grown-ups. This theory has helped nothing in the progress of science. It is useless." According to Dr. T. N. Tahmisian (Atomic Energy Commission), "Scientists who go about teaching that evolution is a fact of life are great con-men, and the story they are telling may be the greatest hoax ever. In explaining evolution, we do not have one iota of fact."

Albert Einstein said, "Science can only be created by those who are thoroughly imbued with the aspiration toward truth and understanding. This source of feeling, however, springs from the sphere of religion. To this there also belongs the faith in the possibility that the regulations valid for the world of existence are rational, that is, comprehensible to reason. I cannot conceive of a genuine scientist without that profound faith."

As with hypocrisy and other issues, don't make evolution a stumbling block when it comes to your salvation. Evolution is a non-issue when it comes to getting right with God. All that God requires of you is that you repent and trust the Savior. Once God transforms you, you will see everything in a new light.

BIRTH NAME: Isaac Hayes
DATE OF BIRTH: August 20, 1942
PLACE OF BIRTH: Covington, Tennessee
OCCUPATIONS: Recording Artist, Actor
CLAIM TO FAME: Theme for *Shaft* (1971)

ISAAC HAYES

I saac Hayes said, "The religion of Scientology is an applied religious philosophy...You apply it. You practice it. Put it in your everyday life, because you use it for life improvement, for enhancing and expanding your spirituality, to make you more able and to promote regained abilities."[215]

In another interview, he said, "Getting into Scientology was the best thing that ever happened to me...It caused me to let things happen. It expands my spirituality, [I'm] more ethical, and when your ethics are in, all kinds of wonderful things happen for you."[216]

BIRTH NAME: Whitney Elizabeth Houston
DATE OF BIRTH: August 9, 1963
PLACE OF BIRTH: Newark, New Jersey
OCCUPATIONS: Singer, Actress, Model
CLAIM TO FAME: Hit album *Whitney Houston* (1985)

WHITNEY HOUSTON

W hen asked about a movie role that dealt with religion, Whitney Houston stated, "Today's time and place is crying for this kind of movie. We didn't think about whether or not it would be accepted as far as talking about God and faith and church and singing the gospel and praises to God and all that stuff."[217]

She said of her religious background, "I'm a human. I was raised as a Baptist. I'm still a Baptist. But I just totally depend on God. I just have faith."[218]

BIRTH NAME: Brian Warner
DATE OF BIRTH: January 5, 1969
PLACE OF BIRTH: Canton, Ohio
OCCUPATION: Musician
CLAIM TO FAME: Shock rocker

MARILYN MANSON

Marilyn Manson, whose parents were Episcopal and Catholic, said, "Initially I was drawn into the darker side of life. But it's really just human nature. I started to learn that everything that's considered a sin is what makes you a human being. All the seven deadly sins are man's true nature."[219]

The above statement is true, but the Bible speaks of far more than *seven* deadly sins that are man's true nature:

> Now the works of the flesh are evident, which are: adultery, fornication, uncleanness, lewdness, idolatry, sorcery, hatred, contentions, jealousies, outbursts of wrath, selfish ambitions, dissensions, heresies, envy, murders, drunkenness, revelries, and the like;...those who practice such things will not inherit the kingdom of God.[220]

Manson attended a nondenominational Christian school, where he "was taught a very underhanded form of Christianity." He explained that his Bible teacher would ask if anyone in the class was

Catholic or Jewish, then "if there was no response, she would talk about how wrong those other religions interpreted the Bible. So at an early age, Christians already started to appear to me as people who believed that their interpretation of God was the only one that was right."

This brings up an interesting point about the exclusive nature of Christianity. I'm not sure what his teacher said, but Christianity isn't anti-Catholic, it simply has *different* teachings from Catholicism—and from much of today's Protestantism. A few minutes' study of the New Testament will make clear the distinction between what the plumb line says and what man's religious traditions say. For example, Jesus said that unless we are "born again," we cannot enter God's Kingdom. This essential aspect of salvation isn't clearly taught by the Catholic church, or even by many mainline Protestant churches.

The New Testament also makes it clear that no one will be spared from God's justice by religious works, yet most contemporary traditional churches teach that all a person must do to enter heaven is believe in God and try to live a good life. This is plainly not what the New Testament teaches.[221]

The issue of your eternal salvation is too important for me to remain harmonious with the chorus of pleasant religious traditions. If what God's Word says is out of line with what humanity teaches, so be it. The plumb line must be our guide.

Manson also insinuated that the brand of Christianity he was taught was somehow anti-Semitic. Since I'm Jewish, I can testify that Christianity is simply born out of Judaism.[222] Psalm 22 speaks of the Messiah having His hands and His feet "pierced," clearly prophesying of the horror of the cross, while Isaiah 53 speaks unmistakably of the suffering Messiah. I don't know how any Jewish person who believes the Scriptures cannot see the identity of the Messiah, and bow at the feet of Jesus of Nazareth.

BIRTH NAME: Robert Urich
DATE OF BIRTH: December 19, 1946
PLACE OF BIRTH: Toronto, Ohio
DATE OF DEATH: April 16, 2002
OCCUPATIONS: Actor, Producer
CLAIM TO FAME: "Vega$" (1978–81)

ROBERT URICH

In answer to the question, "Are you a Christian? Or what is your religion now?" Robert Urich said, "I have always been a Christian. I was baptized and raised Roman Catholic."[223]

Asked if his battle with cancer affected his beliefs, he responded, "Well, I have prayed every day of my life. I think maybe the prayers now are a little more specific. And, I am trying to listen a little more... Every day I ask God to tell me what He really wants me to learn from this."[224]

BIRTH NAME: Denzel Washington
DATE OF BIRTH: December 28, 1954
PLACE OF BIRTH: Mount Vernon, New York
OCCUPATIONS: Actor, Director, Producer
CLAIM TO FAME: "St. Elsewhere" (1982–1988)

DENZEL WASHINGTON

The son of a preacher, Denzel Washington says he is deeply religious and believes every event in his life has been touched by God. "There's no doubt about it—I have felt the hand of God throughout my life... I had that Pentecostal foundation and a mother who used to say, 'Son, you never know who's praying for you.'" He credits prayer for keeping his marriage intact: "I look around and see that very few people have more than 20 years into a marriage...What makes my marriage work? Lots of prayer!" [225]

After he played the role of an angel, he was asked, "Do you believe in angels?" Washington answered, "Yes. I believe in God and the Bible. I believe that we all have angel potentiality as well..." When asked for his life's priorities, he replied, "God, family, work. Football."[226]

BIRTH NAME: Oprah Gail Winfrey
DATE OF BIRTH: January 29, 1954
PLACE OF BIRTH: Kosciusko, Mississippi
OCCUPATIONS: Actress, TV/Radio Host, Producer
CLAIM TO FAME: *The Color Purple* (1985)

OPRAH WINFREY

Oprah Winfrey said, "One of the biggest mistakes humans make is to believe there is only one way. Actually, there are many diverse paths leading to what you call God."[227]

While Oprah Winfrey is likeable, kind, and intelligent, she is in direct conflict with the Bible on this issue. The significant difference between Jesus Christ and all major religions is that He claimed He alone has the power to forgive sin. No religion can offer God the payment that the Moral Law demands. They are self-righteous, trying to earn God's favor with good works or with self-suffering. The Bibles says of them: "For they being ignorant of God's righteousness, and seeking to establish their own righteousness, have not submitted to the righteousness of God. For Christ is the end of the law for righteousness to everyone who believes."[228]

We *cannot* pay for our own sin. But Jesus Christ has already provided the payment through His life's blood. That's why He said, "I am the way, the truth, and the life. No one comes to the Father except through Me."[229]

BIRTH NAME: J. R. Cash
DATE OF BIRTH: February 26, 1932
PLACE OF BIRTH: Kingsland, Arkansas
DATE OF DEATH: September 12, 2003
OCCUPATIONS: Country Music Singer/Songwriter, Actor, Producer
CLAIM TO FAME: Hit single "Man in Black" (1971)

JOHNNY CASH

Known as "The Man in Black," Johnny Cash wrote these lyrics in his trademark song: "I wear the black for those who've never read or listened to the words that Jesus said."

Cash stated, "How well I have learned that there is no fence to sit on between heaven and hell. There is a deep, wide gulf, a chasm, and in that chasm is no place for any man."[230]

After he had been diagnosed with a serious illness, he was asked what he thought was on the other side of the door of death. Cash replied, "I thought it was going to be pretty nice and peaceful on the other side, so I guess maybe that's why I didn't worry about it. I knew it was going to be all right when I got over there...I thought of it in Christian terms—that I would be there with God in eternal bliss. Ecstasy." After laughing, he continued, "I was kind of disappointed when I realized I wasn't going to die—you know, more of this pain! But my faith held up beautifully. I never questioned God, I never doubted God, I never got angry at God. I can't understand people saying they got angry at God. I walked with God all the way through all this. That's why I didn't fear. I never feared anything."[231]

BIRTH NAME: Matthew Raymond Dillon
DATE OF BIRTH: February 18, 1964
PLACE OF BIRTH: New Rochelle, New York
OCCUPATIONS: Actor, Director
CLAIM TO FAME: *My Bodyguard* (1980)

MATT DILLON

When working on a movie about Buddhism, Matt Dillon was given a Buddhist "amulet" by two people working on the film. He said he used the amulet to protect him from fear, and he still wears it. "It reminds me, whenever I'm afraid, to replace it with a faith that things will work out."[232]

He was raised as a Roman Catholic but said he appreciates Buddhism's "rational, informal quality. Coming from my experience of growing up a Catholic, I found Buddhism to be refreshingly easy-going and forgiving."[233]

It is interesting to note that Matt Dillon struggled with the miraculous side of the Bible. He said, "I find myself immediately put off by magical realism...miracles just happening, people walking on water. I struggle with that. I'm convinced that Jesus was a great holy man. He had a great message, but I question the walking on water."[234]

He went on to say, "I pray every day. I don't pray to any specific deity, but that's my thing. That's important."[235]

If Jesus was indeed "a great holy man," then what He said was true. If He lied about Himself even once, then He is neither great nor holy. He instead was a deceiver, and there is therefore nothing "holy" about Him. C. S. Lewis stated it this way: "A man who was merely a man and said the sort of things Jesus said wouldn't be a great moral teacher. He'd either be a lunatic—on a level with the man who says he's a poached egg—or else he'd be the Devil of Hell. You must make your choice. Either this man was, and is, the Son of God: or else a madman or something worse. You can shut Him up for a fool, you can spit at Him and kill Him as a demon; or you can fall at His feet and call Him Lord and God. But don't let us come with any patronizing nonsense about His being a great human teacher. He hasn't left that open to us. He didn't intend to."[236]

BIRTH NAME: William Henry Gates III
DATE OF BIRTH: October 28, 1955
PLACE OF BIRTH: Seattle, Washington
OCCUPATION: Chairman and CEO of Microsoft Corporation
CLAIM TO FAME: Software for Personal Computers

BILL GATES

While not a Hollywood persona, being one of the wealthiest people in the world certainly qualifies Bill Gates for celebrity status. When asked, "Do you believe in the Sermon on the Mount?" Gates replied, "I don't. I'm not somebody who goes to church on a regular basis. The specific elements of Christianity are not something I'm a huge believer in. There's a lot of merit in the moral aspects of religion. I think it can have a very, very positive impact.

"In terms of doing things I take a fairly scientific approach to why things happen and how they happen. I don't know if there's a God or not, but I think religious principles are quite valid."[237]

Again, if we take a "fairly scientific approach" in examining why and how things happen, it is illogical and unscientific to doubt the cause of all things (a Creator).

For instance, we are more than an evolved animal. The Scriptures tell us that animals are created "without understanding." Human beings are different from animals. As we have seen earlier, we are made in God's "image." As human beings, we are aware of our "being." God called Himself "I AM," and we know that "we are." We have understanding that we exist.

Among other unique characteristics, we have an innate ability to appreciate God's creation. What animal gazes with awe at a sunset, or at the magnificence of the Grand Canyon? What animal obtains joy from the sounds of music or takes the time to form an orchestra to create music? What animal among the beasts sets up court systems and apportions justice to its fellow creatures? Only humans are moral beings. While birds and other creatures have instincts to create (nests, etc.), we have the ability to uncover the hidden laws of electricity. We can utilize the law of aerodynamics to transport ourselves around the globe. We also have the God-given ability to appreciate the *value* of creation. We unearth the hidden treasures of gold, silver, diamonds, and oil and make use of them for our own benefit. Only humans have the unique ability to appreciate God for this incredible creation, and to respond to His love.

BIRTH NAME: Lawrence Tureaud
DATE OF BIRTH: May 21, 1952
PLACE OF BIRTH: Chicago, Illinois
OCCUPATIONS: Professional Wrestler, Actor
CLAIM TO FAME: "The A-Team" (1983–1987)

MR. T

Asked about his spiritual upbringing, Mr. T said, "I like to tell everybody that my father baptized me when I was four years old. Even though I was young and couldn't understand a lot of things, but I grew in the church, you know. So when my father wasn't around, my mother was there singing spiritual songs, doing the laundry, so I was constantly being bombarded by good things, you know. So, I'm in church and I'm listening to my father preach...I remember when I used to be outside playing and my father would be praying. I would tiptoe in and that would be so important.

"What was my father doing? He was praying. He was getting the sermon ready for Sunday. He wasn't beating my mother or drinking, he was praying. And that's something special. He taught me to pray. He taught me to have faith, so you know, that's powerful stuff."[238]

BIRTH NAME: Joe Yule Jr.
DATE OF BIRTH: September 23, 1920
PLACE OF BIRTH: New York City, New York
OCCUPATIONS: Actor, Director, Musician
CLAIM TO FAME: *A Family Affair* (1937)

MICKEY ROONEY

Mickey Rooney said, "I've given my life to God, and I try and do the right thing, but inevitably, and unfortunately, I do the wrong thing." He added, "I suffer from being human."[239]

Rooney says he discovered God after an angel, appearing in the form of a busboy with brilliant golden hair, whispered, "Mr. Rooney, Jesus Christ loves you very much." Shook, Rooney discovered that nobody else in the crowded restaurant had seen that busboy. "I realized that the busboy was an angel sent from heaven. He was telling me to clean up my act, straighten up my life and become a good Christian again." Rooney is now a practicing Christian Scientist.[240]

In 1990, Rooney wrote an editorial in which he said, "The on-screen depiction of religion is less than flattering, and, as a Christian,

I pray the era of denigrating religion on screen comes to a screech-ing halt. And soon."[241]

BIRTH NAME: Thomas Cruise Mapother IV
DATE OF BIRTH: July 3, 1962
PLACE OF BIRTH: Syracuse, New York
OCCUPATIONS: Actor, Director, Producer
CLAIM TO FAME: *Risky Business* (1983)

TOM CRUISE

T om Cruise was asked, "What drew you to Scientology? Did you grow up in a faith?" He answered, "Different faiths. Different faiths. And what drew me to it [Scientology]—it was so practical and it just made sense to me, and things that I wanted to figure out in my life..."[242]

Cruise has described Scientology as "an applied religious phi-losophy that you use in your life to help you...It's something that helps an individual find out who you are."[243]

BIRTH NAME: James Patrick Caviezel
DATE OF BIRTH: September 26, 1968
PLACE OF BIRTH: Mount Vernon, Washington
OCCUPATION: Actor
CLAIM TO FAME: *The Thin Red Line* (1998)

JIM CAVIEZEL

J im Caviezel, a Catholic, described the three reactions he ob-served to the "presence" of Jesus while filming *The Passion of the Christ:* "There were people who were indifferent...On the other side were the people who would just love me—they would be in love with Jesus...And last was the complete hatred...There are those who hate the whole idea of Christianity—there are persecutions of other religions as well. But the acknowledgment that you were made by a higher being and then to be so specific, like in our faith, you are open for major ridicule."[244]

Caviezel said someone suggested to him why Jesus spoke in parables: "When you speak this way, it's almost as if God hands you a lamp and you can understand it or you can pretend not to." Caviezel added, "Even though some people said they didn't understand, I believe they did. It was like they were slaughtering His words. God knew their heart; He knew they purposely chose not to understand. He allowed Himself to be the Lamb of God and His words are that way. So the same thing goes with this film—there are going to be a group of people who understand exactly what you mean—and those who understand it but pretend that they misunderstand it."[245]

Caviezel talked of the tremendous pain he endured during filming of the scourging scene, and related it to the reality of what Jesus must have suffered: "I thought, '...If they were hitting Him that hard, how did He breathe?' He experienced a great amount of horrific pain, but also suffocation, which He experienced again on the cross. He was even suffocating while He was carrying the cross. It had to be God. That's what was going through my mind. It has to be God. How could people not know this?"[246]

Did you see *The Passion of the Christ?* As I watched it, my palms began to sweat and I hyperventilated during the crucifixion scene; it was so brutal. When you see a violent movie, the scene is usually over in a moment, but in *The Passion of the Christ* it went on, and on, and on. While there was some "artistic license" taken in the movie, the brutality was based on what Scripture says actually happened to Jesus of Nazareth. It tells us that He was "marred more than any man." He was "bruised for *our* iniquities." Think about what God did for you. He satisfied the requirements of the Law, and He cried out "It is finished!" In other words, He paid the debt for our sins in full. Then He rose from the dead, defeating death forever. The moment we repent and trust the Savior, God forgives our sins and grants us everlasting life.

BIRTH NAME: Ronald Wilson Reagan
DATE OF BIRTH: February 6, 1911
PLACE OF BIRTH: Tampico, Illinois
OCCUPATIONS: Actor, California Governor
CLAIM TO FAME: U.S. President (1981–1989)

RONALD REAGAN

On the first evening after the assassination attempt on his life, Ronald Reagan recommitted his life to God. He wrote these words in his diary: "Whatever happens now, I owe my life to God and will try to serve Him in every way I can." During his recovery, he came to this realization: "Perhaps having come so close to death made me feel I should do whatever I could in the years God had given me to reduce the threat of nuclear war; perhaps there was a reason I had been spared."[247] A short time after this he wrote to Soviet leader Leonid Brezhnev, setting in motion the process leading to the end of the Cold War.

Reagan firmly believed the Lord had spared his life for a reason and had given him a mission to accomplish. Saying "it was only divine intervention that kept me alive," Reagan credited God alone for the many "miraculous factors" that sustained him on that day.

BIRTH NAME: Natalie Maria Cole
DATE OF BIRTH: February 6, 1950
PLACE OF BIRTH: Los Angeles, California
OCCUPATION: Recording Artist
CLAIM TO FAME: Daughter of Nat "King" Cole

NATALIE COLE

Natalie Cole, when asked, "How did you know to call on the name of the Lord?" responded, "Oh please, that's inborn in all of us to call on God. That's the first thing we say: 'Oh, God, help me.' You know, why not? I think that's a part of what He put in us and what we do with the rest of it is a choice we make. I think it is something that everybody knows, about God.

"When you have put all your faith in man and continue to be disappointed, don't you hope there is something out there that is not of human element?"[248]

BIRTH NAME: Barbara Ann Mandrell
DATE OF BIRTH: December 25, 1948
PLACE OF BIRTH: Houston, Texas
OCCUPATIONS: Recording Artist, Actress, Writer, Producer
CLAIM TO FAME: Hit single "Sleeping Single in a Double Bed" (1978)

BARBARA MANDRELL

With so many show business marriages failing, Barbara Mandrell was asked how her marriage has lasted 34 years. She replied, "By our Heavenly Father and only because of God, only because of God...A marriage is three of us."[249]

Barbara said of her outlook on life: "I realize we're not promised tomorrow. Believe me, I realize that. But if God blesses me and lets me stay, I love my life so much, it is such a good life. I am eager to throw myself at His feet…I don't know what the future holds, but I know that God holds tomorrow, so it is exciting. Even when I have hard things happen, He loves me so big, so much. I come through it and I grow from it, because He has got me. He is on the throne. That is why I'm not worried."[250]

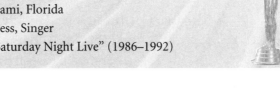

BIRTH NAME: Victoria Jackson
DATE OF BIRTH: August 2, 1959
PLACE OF BIRTH: Miami, Florida
OCCUPATIONS: Actress, Singer
CLAIM TO FAME: "Saturday Night Live" (1986–1992)

VICTORIA JACKSON

Victoria Jackson was asked, "Is religion still a central part of your life?" She replied, "I don't think of the Bible as a 'religion' because the word 'religion' comes from *religio*, which means to 'bind back to God.' Religion is man's attempt to bind himself back to a relationship with God…Most religions teach works for salvation. If you give money, if you go to church, if you crawl on your knees to Mecca, if you say Hail Mary 50 times, if you give us more money or whatever, you'll go to heaven. Basically, most religions say 'Be good and you'll go to heaven'—and that's religion.

"[So] I don't feel any part of religion. I think the Bible is God's gift of salvation that He gave me because I trusted in Him when I was six years old. It was a gift and I didn't earn it."[251]

She explained how her faith has helped her in her career: "If you believe in Christ and that your main goal with your life is supposed to be to honor Him and do His will, then you don't have as much pressure as someone who bases all their happiness on whether they're a movie star."[252]

BIRTH NAME: William Maher
DATE OF BIRTH: January 20, 1956
PLACE OF BIRTH: New York City, New York
OCCUPATIONS: Comedian, TV Host, Producer
CLAIM TO FAME: Host of "Politically Incorrect with Bill Maher"
(1994–2002)

BILL MAHER

When asked the question, "Is there a God?" Bill Maher replied, "I think there is... I'm not an atheist. There's a really big difference between an atheist and someone who just doesn't believe in religion. Religion to me is a bureaucracy between man and God that I don't need. But I'm not an atheist, no. I believe there's some force. If you want to call it God...

"I don't believe God is a single parent who writes books. I think that the people who think God wrote a book called The Bible are just childish. Religion is so childish... These myths, these silly little stories that they believe in fundamentally, that they take over this little space in Jerusalem where one guy flew up to heaven—no, no, this guy performed a sacrifice here a thousand million years ago. It's like, 'Who cares?'"[253]

While Bill Maher is not so foolish as to be an atheist, he does believe people who think God wrote the Bible are childish because it is full of "myths" and "silly little stories." His attitude is understandable and very predictable. It's understandable that you and I can make a wrong (and sometimes unwise) judgment if we don't see the whole picture. Often, all it takes is one piece of information —a missing puzzle piece that enables a picture to make sense.

For example, I recently had dinner at a high-class restaurant in North Carolina. While waiting for the meal to be served, I noticed a large rectangular steel plate sitting right in the middle of the table. It looked out of place, but I didn't want to seem stupid by asking why it was there, so I simply reached out and touched it with my finger. The moment my finger burned, I understood that it was a hot hotplate, heated to keep hot plates hot. Had I noticed the lighted candle under it, I probably wouldn't have been so stupid as to touch it.

Here are some stories that may cause you to make a wrong and unwise judgment: Adam and Eve, Noah's ark, Jonah and the whale, Sampson and Delilah, Moses and the Red Sea, Joshua and the walls of Jericho, Daniel and the lion's den. Do you believe the events in those stories actually happened? Before you answer, let me pass you the missing puzzle piece.

God, in His great wisdom, has deliberately chosen seemingly foolish things to confound those who think they are wise. Who would believe such childish stories? Certainly not those who have any pride or intellectual dignity. God has made the door of salvation so low that only those who are prepared to intellectually humble themselves can enter.

This incredible biblical principle was clearly illustrated years ago when I ran a children's club. I told about one hundred kids to line up for free candy. As I looked at the line, I noticed that the big bullies had pushed their way to the front of the line and the quiet, meek, and sickly children were at the other end. So I told the kids to do an about-face. Then I took great delight in going to the other end of the line and giving candy to the quiet, meek, and sickly kids first.

In a world where bullies push their way to the front, where the rich and powerful stomp on the poor and weak, God has turned the line around. He has chosen seemingly foolish things to confound the wise. He has made it possible for the loser to become a winner, for the underdog to defeat the bully.

Consider the biblical story of Naaman, the proud captain of the Syrian guard. Unfortunately, he developed leprosy, a disease that rendered him "unclean" and destined him to live as an outcast.

Then one day, he heard there was a prophet in Israel who could heal leprosy. So Naaman sought him out, laden with gifts.

When he found him, he waited with his horses and chariot at the prophet's door. But Elisha the prophet didn't even come out of his home. He simply relayed a message saying that the leper should go and wash seven times in the Jordan River and that he would be healed.

Naaman expected that the prophet would at least do him the honor of coming out to greet him, and then wave his regal hand over him in the name of God. Instead, Naaman was told to go bathe in a dirty little river. He was outraged at such stupidity, and angrily rode off on his high horse.

Then his servants reasoned with him and said that if the prophet had told him to do some great thing, he would have done it to be healed. Why not do this simple thing? He had nothing to lose but his dignity. So, having no other course, this proud warrior humbled himself and waded into that dirty little river and bobbed up and down seven times like a rubber ducky.

On the sixth time he went down into the water as a leper, but when he came up after the seventh, we are informed that his skin was like that of a little child. Once again, we see God, in His great consistency, using a foolish and humbling principle.

The Bible tells us that this same principle was used in the redemption of humanity. It says that the message of the cross "is foolishness to those who are perishing."[254] As Bill Maher said, "This guy performed a sacrifice here a thousand million years ago. It's like, 'Who cares?'" The cross makes no sense until another missing puzzle piece comes into play. What is the piece that will make a baffled sinner see the whole picture? It is the Moral Law of God. When the Ten Commandments are placed into their rightful position, the gospel is no longer a mystery; as we recognize our sinfulness before a holy God, we see our need for a Savior. The Law becomes our "tutor" to bring us to Christ.[255]

Think of it: Adam and Eve, Noah's ark, Jonah and the whale, etc., were all genuine events, placed in the Bible to ensnare the proud in their craftiness.[256] How wonderful of God to turn the line around.

I really don't mind being considered a child, because Jesus said that was the only way anyone could enter heaven.[257] Again, Bill Maher's attitude—"the people who think God wrote a book called The Bible are just childish. Religion is so childish"—is predictable.

Here are additional pieces of evidence for the supernatural origin of the Bible, for you to consider:[258]

1. **It is unique in its continuity.** If just 10 people today were picked who were from the same place, born around the same time, spoke the same language, and made about the same amount of money, and were asked to write on just one controversial subject, they would have trouble agreeing with each other. But the Bible stands alone. It was written over a period of 1,600 years by more than 40 writers from all walks of life. Some were fishermen; some were politicians. Others were generals or kings, shepherds or historians. They were from three different continents, and wrote in three different languages. They wrote on hundreds of controversial subjects yet they wrote with agreement and harmony. They wrote in dungeons, in temples, on beaches, and on hillsides, during peacetime and during war. Yet their words sound like they came from the same source. So even though 10 people today couldn't write on one controversial subject and agree, God picked 40 different people to write the Bible —and it has stood the test of time.

2. **It is unique in its circulation**. The invention of the printing press in 1450 made it possible to print books in large quantities. The first book printed was the Bible. Since then, it has been read by more people and printed more times than any other book in history. By 1930, over one billion Bibles had been distributed by Bible societies around the world. By 1977, Bible societies alone were printing over 200 million Bibles each year, and this doesn't include the rest of the Bible publishing companies. No one who is interested in knowing the truth can ignore such an important book.

3. **It is unique in its translation.** The Bible has been translated into over 1,400 languages. No other book even comes close.

4. **It is unique in its survival.** In ancient times, books were copied by hand onto manuscripts that were made from parchment and would decay over time. Ancient books are available today only because someone made copies of the originals to preserve them. For example, the original writings of Julius Caesar are no longer around. We know what he wrote only by the copies we have. Only 10 copies still exist, and they were made 1,000 years after he died. Only 600 copies of Homer's *The Iliad* exist, made 1,300 years after the originals were written. No other book has as many copies of the ancient manuscripts as the Bible. In fact, there are over 24,000 copies of New Testament manuscripts, some from within 35 years of the writer's death.

5. **It is unique in withstanding attack.** No other book has been so attacked throughout history as the Bible. In A.D. 300 the Roman emperor Diocletian ordered every Bible burned because he thought that by destroying the Scriptures he could destroy Christianity. Anyone caught with a Bible would be executed. But just 25 years later, the Roman emperor Constantine ordered that 50 perfect copies of the Bible be made at government expense. The French philosopher Voltaire, a skeptic who destroyed the faith of many people, boasted that within 100 years of his death, the Bible would disappear from the face of the earth. Voltaire died in 1728, but the Bible lives on. The irony of history is that 50 years after his death, the Geneva Bible Society moved into his former house and used his printing presses to print thousands of Bibles. The Bible has also survived criticism. No book has been more attacked for its accuracy. And yet archeologists are proving every year that the Bible's detailed descriptions of historic events are correct.

There is one more piece of the puzzle: the Scriptures tell us that the "natural man" cannot understand the things of the Spirit of God. While the above information may help to convince you intellectually of the inspiration of the Bible, you need more than that to understand it.

Most Americans would find it difficult to understand the Chinese language. However, a child who is *born* into a Chinese family can understand every word. That's why you must be born again with God's Spirit living within you. The moment you become part of God's family, the Scriptures will come alive and begin to make sense.

BIRTH NAME: Richard Tiffany Gere
DATE OF BIRTH: August 31, 1949
PLACE OF BIRTH: Philadelphia, Pennsylvania
OCCUPATIONS: Actor, Producer, Composer
CLAIM TO FAME: *An Officer and a Gentleman* (1982)

RICHARD GERE

Richard Gere stated in an interview, "I was always interested in moral and metaphysical questions: What are the underpinnings of reality? The mind? Where is the soul?" Asked what first attracted him to Buddhism, Gere replied, "The willingness of Buddhism to really attack even the concept of a self: Is there a self?"[259]

Richard said of his spiritual leader, the Dalai Lama, whom he refers to as "His Holiness": "We see him as a spiritual teacher, we see him as a deity."[260] Richard explains how he has been transformed by the teachings of Buddhism: "There is a lot of work on the mind and intellectual play and exploration of reality itself, using language and pure logic, along with various techniques of meditation.

It's a gradual process as the mind is familiarized with another way of seeing things and, hopefully, the correct way. So it is a process that takes several lifetimes, but if within a lifetime one can see gradual change..."[261]

BIRTH NAME: Patricia Heaton
DATE OF BIRTH: March 4, 1958
PLACE OF BIRTH: Cleveland, Ohio
OCCUPATION: Actress
CLAIM TO FAME: "Everybody Loves Raymond" (1996–present)

PATRICIA HEATON

When asked in an interview, "Is there a God?" Patricia Heaton answered, "Oh, yes! The whole thing is about Jesus...He's coming back.[262] Yes. [Laughs.] That's what I'm waiting for. The whole thing revolves around that."[263]

In another interview, she said, "When I was growing up, my home was very Christ-centered...I'm trying to give my children the same thing. I'm not talking about just knowledge...While I feel education is very important, without Christ, education doesn't matter. Wisdom is different from knowledge. You can know a lot, but if your heart isn't focused with Christ at the center, then everything ultimately doesn't work."[264]

She went on to explain, "The point in Christianity is that your life is in submission to God. By the power of His Spirit, the process of our life can be to become like Him—as opposed to having an agenda and hoping if we add God into the mix, He will help us accomplish that. Unfortunately, a lot of people everywhere, and especially in this town, add on some kind of spiritual thing to help their life work better. They make their spirituality a part of their life as opposed to the core. Jesus is not a crutch, though. Jesus must be your life."[265]

BIRTH NAME: Ramon Estevez
DATE OF BIRTH: August 3, 1940
PLACE OF BIRTH: Dayton, Ohio
OCCUPATIONS: Actor, Director, Producer
CLAIM TO FAME: *Badlands* (1973)

MARTIN SHEEN

An interviewer asked, "What is a radical Catholic, as you've called yourself?" Martin Sheen replied, "That is someone who follows the teachings of the nonviolent Jesus and takes the gospel personally, and then pays the price. I fall into that category."[266]

"I never lost my faith," he says. "I was married in church, and I baptized my children. But, like all modern Catholics, I felt for a time that I had outgrown the church. Now it is a bone of contention in my soul that I did not share my faith with my kids, as my parents did with me. It was a source of grace when I needed it. I have been greatly nurtured and inspired by my faith."[267]

It seems a bit odd that someone would refer to "the nonviolent Jesus." There is only one Jesus. We cannot pick and choose which character traits we like and then create a Jesus who differs from the one revealed to us in the Bible. While shaping a Savior that fits a nonviolent agenda may seem commendable, the Jesus of the Scriptures was at times violent. He took a whip in His strong carpenter's hand, violently overturned the tables of the moneychangers (televangelists of His day), and no doubt used the whip to clear them out of the temple.

Jesus on occasion also condemned certain people for their sin. In Matthew 23 He called the religious leaders "hypocrites" seven times. He told them that they were "blind fools," children of hell, full of hypocrisy and sin. He climaxed His sermon by saying, "Serpents, brood of vipers! How can you escape the condemnation of hell?" He then warned that He would say to the wicked, "Depart from Me, you cursed, into the everlasting fire prepared for the devil and his angels."[268] And the Bible tells of a future time "when the Lord Jesus is revealed from heaven with His mighty angels, in flaming fire taking vengeance on those who do not know God, and on those who do not obey the gospel of our Lord Jesus Christ. These shall be punished with everlasting destruction from the presence of the Lord and from the glory of His power."[269] That doesn't sound "nonviolent."

Even if our motives are sincere, it is unethical to consider just the portions of a man's life that we like, and to shape them to fit what we think he should be like. Yet this is a common practice for those who use religion for political or social causes.

Despite attempts to reshape Him, we are told of the Savior, "Jesus Christ is the same yesterday, today, and forever."[270]

BIRTH NAME: Allan See
DATE OF BIRTH: February 28, 1930
PLACE OF BIRTH: Mount Kisco, New York
OCCUPATION: Actor
CLAIM TO FAME: "Mary Tyler Moore Show" (1970–1977)

GAVIN MCLEOD

In an interview Gavin McLeod told how he and his wife, Patti, had divorced, but God miraculously intervened and they both found Christ and were remarried. McLeod explained, "I put my work before my wife and I didn't know about priority systems. I was completely unbalanced and as a result the marriage was shaky and I was not committed. But when you put Christ first in your life, your wife second, then your family and your work and the church, then you have a balance." He gives this advice to those whose marriages are struggling: "I would suggest that you realize that God is the most important thing in everyone's life..."[271]

BIRTH NAME: Rosanne Teresa O'Donnell
DATE OF BIRTH: March 21, 1962
PLACE OF BIRTH: Commack, New York
OCCUPATIONS: Actress, Comedian, TV Host
CLAIM TO FAME: Host of "Stand-Up Spotlight" (1988)

ROSIE O'DONNELL

In answer to an inquiry about her Irish Catholic background, Rosie O'Donnell said, "Yes...we were the kind of parish council family. My mother was president of the parish council. We were—we went to Catholic schools."[272]

Presumably in reference to the rampant homosexuality and pedophilia within the Roman Catholic church, her interviewer said, "Now our church finds itself in the worst scandal in its history. I'm having trouble processing all of this." O'Donnell replied, "Maybe, you know, we can melt down some of the gold toilets in the pope's Vatican and pay off some of the lawsuits because, you know, frankly, the whole tenet of Christianity, of being pious, of living a Christ-like life, has been lost in Catholicism, I believe."[273]

Asked whether she was raising her kids Catholic, O'Donnell answered, "No...I don't bring our kids to church at all. But it's funny, because my seven-year-old is overtly spiritual and connects —he got a toddler Bible...And he says to me at night, '...What do you think, Mom, Old Testament or New Testament?' I go, 'You know what, Clark? I don't know the difference.' He goes, 'Old Testament is before the birth of Jesus Christ. You know, the rainbow is God's promise to Noah?' The kid is, like, channeling some sort of Billy Graham!...You know, every time he sees anything related to the Bible, he's—it's pretty amazing."[274]

BIRTH NAME: Kevin Michael Costner
DATE OF BIRTH: January 18, 1955
PLACE OF BIRTH: Lynwood, California
OCCUPATIONS: Actor, Producer, Director
CLAIM TO FAME: *Field of Dreams* (1989)

KEVIN COSTNER

Regarding a role he played in a movie, Kevin Costner was asked, "Did it change the way you believe or have an effect on your faith?" Kevin replied, "Well, I have always wanted to believe that there is something more to life than what we have here on earth. I could relate with what [the character] was going through and the questions he was asking, so in that sense, it did affect me. I mean, it would be nice to know that there is something more, a higher power waiting for us, wouldn't it?"[275]

Asked if he believed in heaven, he replied, "I desperately want to! I mean, I really want to believe that a part of me will continue on after this life and that there's more to me and to this life than just what's here on Earth. Yes, I want to believe."[276]

BIRTH NAME: Goldie Jeanne Hawn
DATE OF BIRTH: November 21, 1945
PLACE OF BIRTH: Washington, D.C.
OCCUPATIONS: Actress, Producer
CLAIM TO FAME: "Rowan & Martin's Laugh-In" (1968–1970)

GOLDIE HAWN

Like Richard Gere and a number of other high-profile Hollywood celebrities, Goldie Hawn is a follower of the Dalai Lama. She first met Tibet's exiled spiritual leader in the early 1990s.

"Being with him, one feels completely at peace," she said.[277] A self-described "Jewish Buddhist," Goldie regularly visits India and spends time with the Dalai Lama.

She observed, "[India] is a fascinating country with such extremes that it never ceases to amaze me. But I wish Indian women would get more respect, apart from reducing the gap between the rich and poor here."[278]

BIRTH NAME: Vincent Damon Furnier
DATE OF BIRTH: February 4, 1948
PLACE OF BIRTH: Detroit, Michigan
OCCUPATIONS: Musician, Singer, Actor
CLAIM TO FAME: The original shock-rocker (1970s)

ALICE COOPER

Alice Cooper, who sang about necrophilia and chopped up baby dolls during his concerts, said that although he continues to record and tour with a theatrical horror-style show, "My life is dedicated to follow Christ." The 56-year-old performer, who says he became a Christian in the 1980s, spoke candidly about his love for God and his reluctance to become a "Christian celebrity." Despite being credited with paving the way for performers such as Marilyn Manson, Alice Cooper was always insulted whenever he was accused of being satanic. He was raised in a Christian home and believed in God, although he was not committed.

That changed when alcoholism threatened his marriage. He and his wife, Sheryl, attended a church with a "hellfire pastor." Cooper said he became a Christian "initially more out of the fear of God, rather than the love of God...I did not want to go to hell."[279]

"I've had a couple of people that were friends of mine that I've talked to that have vocally said they have [accepted Christ]. I have talked to some big stars about this, some really horrific characters

...and you'd be surprised. The ones that you would think are the furthest gone are the ones that are more apt to listen."[280]

Cooper's change of heart is seen in his recent recordings. In performances now he tells people, "Be careful! Satan is not a myth. Don't sit around pretending like Satan is just a joke." To answer his critics, Cooper says, "I was one thing at one time, and I'm something new. I'm a new creature now. Don't judge Alice by what he used to be. Praise God for what I am now."[281]

BIRTH NAME: Michael Andrew Fox
DATE OF BIRTH: June 9, 1961
PLACE OF BIRTH: Edmonton, Alberta, Canada
OCCUPATIONS: Actor, Director, Producer
CLAIM TO FAME: "Family Ties" (1982–1989)

MICHAEL J. FOX

In an interview about his battle with Parkinson's disease Michael J. Fox said, "I just feel like I've been in God's pocket for so long. I just didn't think that I was going to be hammered with this. That I would find a way to live with it, to learn from it and deal with it. And I have."[282]

Although initially devastated at the diagnosis, he said, "I never had a moment where I fell to my knees and said..., 'Oh, God, this is horrible.' You know, 'Why has Thou forsaken me? What is this?' I never had that moment. What I had was, 'Wow. Okay. That's not what I was expecting.'"[283]

At one point Fox underwent a brain operation. Asked whether he was afraid, he replied, "I had full faith in my doctors, and I had full faith in God."[284]

As a result of this disease, his vision of life has also been altered. "It's made me stronger. A million times wiser. And more compassionate," Fox said. "I've realized I'm vulnerable, that no matter how many awards I'm given or how big my bank account is, I can be messed with like that. The end of the story is you die. We all die."[285]

No doubt many were moved to tears when Michael J. Fox began his battle with Parkinson's disease, and asked the question, "Why is there suffering anyway?" Perhaps some concluded, "That proves there is no 'loving' God." Let's consider this important concept.

Study the soil for a moment. It naturally produces weeds. No one plants them; no one waters them. They even stubbornly push through cracks of a dry sidewalk. Millions of useless weeds sprout like there's no tomorrow, strangling our crops and ruining our lawns. Pull them out by the roots, and there will be more tomorrow. They are nothing but a curse.

Consider how much of the earth is uninhabitable. There are *millions* of square miles of barren deserts in Africa and other parts of the world. Most of Australia is nothing but miles and miles of useless desolate land. Not only that, but the earth is constantly shaken with massive earthquakes. Its shores are lashed with hurricanes; tornadoes rip through creation with incredible fury; devastating floods soak the land; and terrible droughts parch the soil. Sharks, tigers, lions, snakes, spiders, and disease-carrying mosquitoes attack humanity and suck its life's blood. The earth's inhabitants are afflicted with disease, pain, suffering, and death.

Think of how many people are plagued with cancer, multiple sclerosis, Alzheimer's, heart disease, emphysema, Parkinson's (like Fox), and a number of other debilitating illnesses. Consider all the children with leukemia, or people born with crippling diseases or without the mental capability to even feed themselves. All these things should convince thinking minds that something is radically wrong. Did God blow it when He created humanity? What sort of tyrant must our Creator be if this was His master plan?

Sadly, many use the issue of suffering as an excuse to reject any thought of God, when its existence is the *very reason* we should accept Him. Suffering stands as terrible testimony to the truth of the explanation given by the Word of God. The Bible is the supernatural testament of our Creator about why there is suffering…and what we can do about it.

The Bible tells us that God cursed the earth because of Adam's disobedience (sin). Weeds *are* a curse. So is disease. Sin and suffering cannot be separated. Again, the Scriptures inform us that we live in a *fallen* creation. In the beginning, God created man perfect, and he lived in a perfect world without suffering. The original creation was "good" and was not filled with violence and bloodshed. *It was heaven on earth.* When sin came into the world, death and misery came with it.

But the day will come when the entire creation will be delivered from the "bondage of corruption" and there will be no more curse. In that coming Kingdom, in the new heaven and new earth, there will be no more pain, suffering, disease, or death. We are told that no eye has ever seen, nor has any ear heard, nor has anyone ever imagined the wonderful things that God has in store for those who love Him.[286] Think for a moment what it would be like if food grew with the fervor of weeds. Consider how wonderful it would be if the deserts became incredibly fertile, if creation stopped devouring itself and humanity. Imagine if the weather worked *for* us instead of against us, if disease completely disappeared, if pain was a thing of the past, if death was no more.

The dilemma is that we are like a child whose insatiable appetite for chocolate has caused his face to break out with ugly sores. He looks in the mirror and sees a sight that makes him depressed. But instead of giving up his beloved chocolate, he consoles himself by stuffing more into his mouth. Yet, the source of his pleasure is actually the *cause* of his suffering.

The whole face of the earth is nothing but ugly sores of suffering. Everywhere we look we see unspeakable pain. But instead of believing God's explanation and asking Him to forgive us and change our appetite, we console ourselves by feeding on sin's sweet delicacies. There we find solace in its temporal pleasures, thus intensifying our pain, both in this life and in the life to come.

BIRTH NAME: Andrew Samuel Griffith
DATE OF BIRTH: June 1, 1926
PLACE OF BIRTH: Mount Airy, North Carolina
OCCUPATIONS: Actor, Producer, Writer, Singer
CLAIM TO FAME: "The Andy Griffith Show" (1960–1968)

ANDY GRIFFITH

In reference to his painful experience with Guillain-Barré syndrome, Andy Griffith said, "I firmly believe that in every situation, no matter how difficult, God extends grace greater than the hardship, and strength and peace of mind that can lead us to a place higher than where we were before."[287]

Griffith developed a love for gospel songs at a young age. When he was a child in Sunday school, he said, "I would sing 'Jesus Loves Me' so loud that everybody would notice."[288]

BIRTH NAME: Charles Eugene Patrick Boone
DATE OF BIRTH: June 1, 1934
PLACE OF BIRTH: Jacksonville, Florida
OCCUPATIONS: Singer/Songwriter, Actor, Author
CLAIM TO FAME: Hit single "Ain't That a Shame" (1955)

PAT BOONE

Pat Boone said of his upbringing, "I was raised in a Christian home. We were at church services every Sunday morning, Sunday night, Wednesday night and every time there was a revival meeting we'd be in every service . . . I didn't want to do something just because it was expected of me. I wanted to understand and appreciate, know what I was doing.

"So I was doing my own Bible reading, my own thinking and came across the passage where Jesus said, 'If any man confesses me before men, I'll confess him before my Father and if he denies me, I'll have to deny him.' I realized even as a 13-year-old, that's the most important thing of my whole existence. So I did that..." He recalled that he spent the next several years "just talking to the Lord and asking him to use my life and direct it and make me useful to him."[289]

BIRTH NAME: Winona Laura Horowitz
DATE OF BIRTH: October 29, 1971
PLACE OF BIRTH: Winona, Minnesota
OCCUPATIONS: Actress, Writer, Producer
CLAIM TO FAME: *Lucas* (1986)

WINONA RYDER

Winona Ryder said about her latest movie, "It touches on things that I'm not sure where I stand on in my own life. Things—God and faith—things that I think when you're in your 20s you're sort of still figuring out where you stand, so in the film I play a woman of devout faith. A woman who really believes in God and the devil, and it's very kind of far from where I'm at in my life. I certainly believe in energies and stuff like that, but I don't believe in the devil."[290]

In speaking of her parents, she said that they "taught me about all different kinds of religion. They just didn't say for me to lean towards any specific one. My mom was very Buddhist, so that was probably the biggest influence on me when I was growing up. I went to Buddhist schools when I was young...I did not grow up with the fear of God—I'll put it that way...But I appreciate all different religions, and I think you should take what you can from each one of them and make up your own."[291]

BIRTH NAME: Kathryn Lee Epstein
DATE OF BIRTH: August 16, 1953
PLACE OF BIRTH: Paris, France
OCCUPATIONS: Actress, TV Co-host
CLAIM TO FAME: "Name That Tune" (1974)

KATHIE LEE GIFFORD

Kathie Lee Gifford, when asked about where she gets her energy, replied, "What most people perceive as energy is really strength of spirit. It comes from the joy of knowing God, loving Him, and being loved by Him."[292]

The most important Christmas tradition in their home is bringing out a cake with candles. Gifford wants her kids to know that Christmas is a joyous celebration of Jesus' birthday. She said, "Jesus was God's gift to the world. I believe that with all my heart."[293]

BIRTH NAME: Mary Jean Tomlin
DATE OF BIRTH: September 1, 1939
PLACE OF BIRTH: Detroit, Michigan
OCCUPATIONS: Actress, Comedian
CLAIM TO FAME: "Rowan & Martin's Laugh-In" (1969–1970)

LILY TOMLIN

Lily Tomlin philosophically said, "Why is it that when we talk to God we're said to be praying, but when God talks to us we're schizophrenic?"[294]

That's actually a good question. Even though it is obviously rhetorical, it deserves an answer. While the Bible speaks of *hearing* God's voice, it is usually "heard" through His Word. We speak to

God through prayer, and He speaks to us through the Scriptures. The psalmist said, "Your word is a lamp to my feet and a light to my path."[295] God, through the Bible, will give you direction regarding what He wants you to do. That's why reading the Scriptures should be a daily habit.

BIRTH NAME: Kirk Thomas Cameron
DATE OF BIRTH: October 12, 1970
PLACE OF BIRTH: Canoga Park, California
OCCUPATION: Actor
CLAIM TO FAME: "Growing Pains" (1985–1992)

KIRK CAMERON

Kirk Cameron said of his days before he became a Christian, "As far as I was concerned, *thinking* people didn't believe in fairy tales." When asked about God, he would say, "There's no God. You can't prove that there's a God. Absolutely not. You guys are performing your own lobotomy in order to believe this kind of stuff."[296]

Through a series of circumstances, he found himself in a church service. He said, "I left the church with my head filled with questions. I felt guilty when [the pastor] talked about sin." The thought occurred to him that if he were to die in a car crash that day, he wouldn't go to heaven. Cameron said he realized, "This is too important. I don't want to be wrong about all this. I prayed the clumsiest prayer that's probably ever been prayed...I said, 'God, if You are there, please show me. If You are real, I need to know.'"[297]

He then started studying the Scriptures. "I couldn't get enough of the Bible," he recalls. "I read about this amazing God who sees my thought-life, who considers lust to be adultery, who considers hatred to be murder, who sees all the sins that I've committed that no one else knows about—the secret arrogant attitudes. And instead of giving me what I deserved, He's provided a way for me to be forgiven and changed."[298]

BIRTH NAME: Britney Jean Spears
DATE OF BIRTH: December 2, 1981
PLACE OF BIRTH: Kentwood, Louisiana
OCCUPATIONS: Singer, Actress
CLAIM TO FAME: Hit single "Baby One More Time" (1999)

BRITNEY SPEARS

Britney Spears said, "I realized that if you can't have fun, why do what you're doing? And my priorities have changed a little bit, too. In that I love what I do, but it's not my life. My family, my God and my boyfriend: That's my life. I do this because I enjoy it...

"I don't want to be scared. I can't walk on pins and needles. So I just have to pray. I just have to pray every night."[299]

BIRTH NAME: Dean Jones
DATE OF BIRTH: January 25, 1931
PLACE OF BIRTH: Decatur, Alabama
OCCUPATIONS: Singer, Actor
CLAIM TO FAME: Disney's *That Darn Cat* (1965)

DEAN JONES

Dean Jones explained what happened when he was first challenged by Christianity: "Once you've heard the truth, and once the reality of Christ is seeded in your heart, it spoils you for joyful sinning. But it was too late. I could only grit my teeth and go forward, hell-bent for leather in spite of the truth that was lodged in my heart...When I surrendered everything to the Lord, the peace of Christ rolled over me like an ocean wave."[300]

He added, "When I was born again, it just ended my career. I was making two pictures a year [he had appeared in more than 40 movies], then didn't work for eleven years. But at some point you have to give up your pride and what other people think about you. The fear of men's faces is a snare and a trap."

Look what has happened. A little town named Hollywood—despite being founded by Christians—in time became corrupt as it promoted its godless industry. It managed to deceive much of the nation into thinking that America was godless. This in turn influenced the removal of the Ten Commandments and prayer from public places.

Yet underneath this black veil, a few of its stars were silently twinkling with their faith in God. They sometimes let out a whisper of this in interviews, no doubt with an eye on their managers for fear of doing what is anathema in the entertainment industry—mentioning God and the movies in the same breath.

This sword of deception that Hollywood has held over America for so many years has a sharp double edge. While they have been deceiving, they have also been deceived. Arnold Schwarzenegger was right when he spoke of forces of evil as being very real. The Scriptures say that the god of this world (Satan) has blinded the minds of those who don't believe.[301] All the while they thought they were spreading their own agenda of violence, blasphemy, and immorality, they were in reality spreading his. They were "taken captive by him to do his will."[302]

Two months after the release of *The Passion of the Christ*, Hollywood was still reeling at its box office success. Think of it. This is a movie about Jesus Christ, the One who is light itself—the One whose name had been incessantly blasphemed by Hollywood.

It is almost humorous to think that the movie isn't even in English; it has *subtitles*. This is America, not some foreign country that doesn't speak English. And it isn't just a religious movie, it is about Jesus Christ. This is about Christianity, the exclusive and despised religion about which a certain CBS anchorman has continually attempted to sow seeds of doubt as to its credibility. His programs repeatedly question the reliability of the historical record—the New Testament itself. I don't think he would be so insensitive to the beliefs of Muslims by questioning the reliability of the Koran; he wouldn't dare because it would put his life in jeopardy.

This movie had everything against it. Yet it exploded out of the box office right into the bank, proving that despite the concerted effort of Hollywood to portray Christians as fools and hypocrites, the country is not anti-God.

Entertainment programs reported its stunning success, and one even questioned why there were so few genuine believers in Hollywood. They concluded that it just wasn't "hip" for those in the entertainment industry to believe in Jesus Christ. What exactly does that mean?

There are a number of reasons why believing in Jesus isn't hip. If a script calls for a sex scene, that's what has to happen. The actor has little say unless he's a mega-star. He certainly can't change a script just because it conflicts with his moral convictions. He's the employee, not the boss. If he refuses to compromise his convictions, he immediately gains the reputation of being a troublemaker. Troublemakers are not good for the bottom line and therefore not good for business—they waste time and cost big money.

So Christian actors have a choice. Either they can compromise and do movies that are filled with blasphemy, sex, and violence, or they can refuse roles and find fewer and fewer offers coming their way.

Of course, being a Christian isn't hip in Hollywood. How could it be? The very nature of the industry is self-promotion. Dean Jones summed it up by saying, "In Hollywood, self is on the throne. The culture of Hollywood encourages it." People who want to be in front of the camera are usually a special breed. They are talented, good-looking, and confident; they are self-sufficient, self-promoting, and intelligent. They don't function like average folk. They want to be seen. They love and live for applause. They want to be famous, and most seem unashamed to admit that they have rather large egos. They epitomize everything Christianity is not.

The apostle Paul addresses this attitude with the Corinthian church. He says, "For you see your calling, brethren, that not many wise according to the flesh, not many mighty, not many noble, are called. But God has chosen the foolish things of the world to put to shame the wise, and God has chosen the weak things of the world to put to shame the things which are mighty; and the base things of the world and the things which are despised God has chosen, and the things which are not, to bring to nothing the things that are, that no flesh should glory in His presence."[303]

Jesus made a similar statement: "I thank You, Father, Lord of heaven and earth, that You have hidden these things from the wise and prudent and revealed them to babes."[304]

In the blockbuster movie *Indiana Jones and the Last Crusade*, Indiana was in search of the Holy Grail. This is supposedly the cup from which Jesus drank at the Last Supper. Whoever sipped from it would receive everlasting life. Through a series of circumstances, Indiana was forced to make his way past three "challenges."

He has clues written in a book that he holds in his hand. As he makes his way toward the Grail, his first clue is "The penitent man will pass." He repeats the words over and over. Suddenly the clue dawns on him. He whispers, "The penitent man is *humble before God…kneel!*" He instantly drops to his knees, and as he does so, two spinning blades slice the air where his head had just been. He has made it past the first challenge.

The second is a group of steppingstones with letters of the alphabet on them. The clue is "Proceed in the footsteps of the Word of God." Again, he says the clue repeatedly. Then he whispers, "The name of God is Jehovah," and takes his first step, almost falling to his death as the steppingstone gives way. He then realizes that the name of God in Latin begins with the letter "I." He steps it out and successfully completes the second challenge.

The third challenge is to pass over a huge, bottomless chasm—with no bridge. The clue given is "The path of God. Only a leap from a lion's head will prove his worth." Indiana is understandably terrified at the thought of stepping off the edge over a deep crevasse when there is nothing upon which to step. But he has no choice. He must stand by the stone carving of the lion's head and take a leap of faith. He closes his eyes and steps out onto nothing.

Suddenly his foot touches something solid. The camera angle moves to one side, revealing that the path upon which he had stepped was optically invisible. He walks across the path and then scoops up some sand to toss back onto it, so that those following might see the way more clearly. He has passed the third challenge.

He approaches a table upon which more than a dozen ancient cups are sitting. Most are made of gold or silver. Which one is the Holy Grail? A knight holding a sword tells him that he must choose. He says, "Choose wisely. The true Grail will give you life. The false grail will take it from you." Those who drink from the wrong cup will find that the curse of the Genesis Fall will take place in seconds, rather than the lifetime it normally takes to age and then die.

Indiana ignores the *golden* cups, picks up a plain one and says, "The cup of a carpenter…" He sips from the cup, and lives. The knight smiles and says, "You have chosen wisely."

Although this captivating story is fiction, it echoes the gospel truth. There is only *one way* to approach God, and that is through bowing the knee. God resists the proud and gives grace to the humble. If you refuse to humble yourself before God, you will suffer swift and terrible consequences. These are not my thoughts; they are the clues, the pointers, the indications from the Book that says it is a lamp to our feet and a light to our path.

The second clue was the name of God. The Book tells us that God has given Jesus a name that is above every other name. It warns, "There is no other name under heaven given among men, whereby we must be saved."[305] *He* is the way, the truth, and the life.[306] It couldn't be clearer. The Bible spells it out for us—so be careful where you step.

Now you stand before the great chasm of eternity. You know that you have to humble yourself. You know the only name that can save you. Now you must take a step of faith to prepare for eternity, for without faith it is impossible to please God.[307] Are you fearful to take that step? You have no choice. Death could seize upon you before you finish reading this sentence...and then you will find yourself in eternity, standing guilty before a Holy God, without a Savior.

Remember that God has "hidden these things from the wise and prudent." What is hidden from your eyes at the moment will be revealed to you *after you have taken that step*. I took it more than thirty years ago and it proved trustworthy. It is a narrow way, but one in which the Lord will uphold you with His hand. Through this publication I am trying my best to make the way apparent for you, so that you can see the path more clearly.

After that step is taken, you may drink from the Cup of Salvation. It isn't made with gold or silver. Nor is it the cold cup of a dead, rich, ritualistic religion. It is a lowly Carpenter's cup—the way of humility and faith, given by the One who said, "Blessed are those who...thirst for righteousness."[308]

Being a Christian means identifying with something Hollywood despises—righteousness. But the way of righteousness is the way to everlasting life.[309] There is no other way. So for a celebrity to publicly come to Christ means that he identifies with righteousness, and that almost certainly means an end to his life as a successful star. That's why it is not "hip" to be a Christian in Hollywood.

BIRTH NAME: Jesus of Nazareth
DATE OF BIRTH: Around 2–6 B.C.
PLACE OF BIRTH: Bethlehem, Judea
DATE OF DEATH: N/A
OCCUPATIONS: Carpenter, Teacher
CLAIM TO FAME: Son of God

JESUS OF NAZARETH

Many years ago, as two skeptics walked the streets of London gazing upon the church steeples, they decided to devote their lives to disproving the myth of Christianity.

One of those men determined that he would do so by studying the New Testament. After two years of reading it, he dropped to his knees and said to Jesus of Nazareth, "My Lord and my God."

That man was General Lew Wallis, and he went on to write the book *Ben-Hur* which was then made into the epic film *Ben-Hur— A Tale of Christ*, winner of eleven Academy Awards.

If you are willing, you will be faced with a challenge similar to the one that confronted this general. We are going to put Jesus of Nazareth on trial for the crime of blasphemy. This is a very serious accusation, one that demands the death of the guilty. Rather than devoting two years to the effort, all I'm asking is that you take 20 minutes or so of your time to consider the evidence.

There will be three players in this court case. I will serve as the defense, presenting what I consider to be evidence that this Man is not guilty of the charge. I maintain that He is actually Almighty God in human form, and that His words are therefore true.

My principal evidence will be a 2,000-year-old exhibit—excerpts from an ancient manuscript. It is the written deposition of the apostle John (an ex-fisherman), and is commonly called "The Gospel of John." One or two of these excerpts are rather long, but please be patient, and don't skip over them as they are very relevant to the case.

I will not draw on the testimony of the miraculous, but will confine myself to the recorded words of Jesus and surrounding relevant verses. We will let His own words condemn or justify Him. There will be no "insanity" plea.

You are to be the second player in this unique trial. I'm going to ask you to play the role of the judge. The only condition is that you must be *completely* impartial. Your challenge is to simply and honestly weigh the given evidence, then make a truthful judgment—innocent or guilty as charged.

The third player in this trial will be the prosecutor. He is the god of this world. He is called the "accuser" and the "father of lies."[310] How will you hear his voice? He will simply speak to you through your mind. That is his territory. You will hear his whisperings, but don't make any judgments until both sides have laid out their evidence.

Let me now begin to build my case. Jesus of Nazareth is speaking:

> "For the Father judges no one, but has committed all judgment to the Son, that all should honor the Son just as they honor the Father. He who does not honor the Son does not honor the Father who sent Him. Most assuredly, I say to you, he who hears My word and believes in Him who sent Me has everlasting life, and shall not come into judgment, but has passed from death into life. Most assuredly, I say to you, the hour is coming, and now is, when the dead will hear the voice of the Son of God; and those who hear will live.
>
> "For as the Father has life in Himself, so He has granted the Son to have life in Himself, and has given Him authority to execute judgment also, because He is the Son of Man. Do not marvel at this; for the hour is coming in which all who are in the graves will hear His voice and come forth;

those who have done good, to the resurrection of life, and those who have done evil, to the resurrection of condemnation." (John 5:22–29)

Much of what Jesus said could be dismissed as simply the radical teachings of an intelligent man. His statements often astounded His hearers because His philosophies were so profound. But consider His words in the above passage carefully. Think about His claims: He said that God Himself had appointed Him as the Judge of all mankind. Humanity should honor Him as much as they honor the Father. Those who didn't honor Him didn't honor God. All who heard His words and trusted in Him escape the wrath of the Law and passed from death to life. The hour would come when *everyone* in the grave would hear His voice and be raised from the dead. Jesus is saying that the entire human race will be raised by His voice, and that they will stand before Him in Judgment.

If you are tempted to think that the Man was completely insane, bear in mind that the life of this one person was so profound that He split time in two. When people heard Him speak, they marveled at His wise words and His life philosophy. He dazzled even the temple teachers with His wisdom. Two thousand years later, millions drink in His words as if they were life itself.

Philip Schaff wrote of Him, "This Jesus of Nazareth, without money and arms, conquered more millions than Alexander, Caesar, Mohammed, and Napoleon; without science and learning, He shed more light on things human and divine than all philosophers and scholars combined; without the eloquence of schools, He spoke such words of life as were never spoken before or since, and produced effects which lie beyond the reach of orator or poet; without writing a single line, He set more pens in motion, and furnished themes for more sermons, orations, discussions, learned volumes, works of art, and songs of praise than the whole army of great men of ancient and modern times."[311]

Even Napoleon Bonaparte admitted, "I know men and I tell you that Jesus Christ is no mere man. Between Him and every other person in the world there is no possible term of comparison. Alexander, Caesar, Charlemagne, and I have founded empires. But on what did we rest the creations of our genius? Upon force. Jesus Christ founded His empire upon love; and at this hour millions of men would die for Him."[312]

Keep those thoughts in mind as you read the following. The next bit of evidence we will consider takes place just after Jesus had fed a great multitude with five loaves and two fish:

> Jesus answered them and said, "Most assuredly, I say to you, you seek Me, not because you saw the signs, but because you ate of the loaves and were filled. Do not labor for the food which perishes, but for the food which endures to everlasting life, which the Son of Man will give you, because God the Father has set His seal on Him." Then they said to Him, "What shall we do, that we may work the works of God?" Jesus answered and said to them, "This is the work of God, that you believe in Him whom He sent." Therefore they said to Him, "What sign will You perform then, that we may see it and believe You? What work will You do? Our fathers ate the manna in the desert; as it is written, 'He gave them bread from heaven to eat.'"
>
> Then Jesus said to them, "Most assuredly, I say to you, Moses did not give you the bread from heaven, but My Father gives you the true bread from heaven. For the bread of God is He who comes down from heaven and gives life to the world." Then they said to Him, "Lord, give us this bread always."
>
> And Jesus said to them, "I am the bread of life. He who comes to Me shall never hunger, and he who believes in Me shall never thirst. But I said to you that you have seen Me and yet do not believe. All that the Father gives Me will

come to Me, and the one who comes to Me I will by no means cast out. For I have come down from heaven, not to do My own will, but the will of Him who sent Me. This is the will of the Father who sent Me, that of all He has given Me I should lose nothing, but should raise it up at the last day. And this is the will of Him who sent Me, that everyone who sees the Son and believes in Him may have everlasting life; and I will raise him up at the last day."

The Jews then complained about Him, because He said, "I am the bread which came down from heaven." And they said, "Is not this Jesus, the son of Joseph, whose father and mother we know? How is it then that He says, 'I have come down from heaven'?" Jesus therefore answered and said to them, "Do not murmur among yourselves. No one can come to Me unless the Father who sent Me draws him; and I will raise him up at the last day. It is written in the prophets, 'And they shall all be taught by God.' Therefore everyone who has heard and learned from the Father comes to Me. Not that anyone has seen the Father, except He who is from God; He has seen the Father.

"Most assuredly, I say to you, he who believes in Me has everlasting life. I am the bread of life. Your fathers ate the manna in the wilderness, and are dead. This is the bread which comes down from heaven, that one may eat of it and not die. I am the living bread which came down from heaven. If anyone eats of this bread, he will live forever; and the bread that I shall give is My flesh, which I shall give for the life of the world."

The Jews therefore quarreled among themselves, saying, "How can this Man give us His flesh to eat?" Then Jesus said to them, "Most assuredly, I say to you, unless you eat the flesh of the Son of Man and drink His blood, you have no life in you. Whoever eats My flesh and drinks My blood has eternal life, and I will raise him up at the last day. For My flesh is food indeed, and My blood is drink indeed. He who eats My flesh and drinks My blood abides in Me, and I in him. As the living Father sent Me, and I live because of the Father, so he who feeds on Me will live because of Me. This is the bread which came down from heaven; not as your fathers ate the manna, and are dead. He who eats this bread will live forever."

These things He said in the synagogue as He taught in Capernaum. Therefore many of His disciples, when they heard this, said, "This is a hard saying; who can understand it?" When Jesus knew in Himself that His disciples complained about this, He said to them, "Does this offend you? What then if you should see the Son of Man ascend where He was before? It is the Spirit who gives life; the flesh profits nothing. The words that I speak to you are spirit, and they are life." (John 6:26–63)

He now claims to be the sustenance of life itself. Again He affirms His pre-existence—that He "came down from heaven," and that He will raise the dead on the last day. Then He gets really bizarre and says that if they want everlasting life they have to eat His flesh and drink His blood! When His hearers were understandably offended by such talk, He said they would change their minds if they saw Him rise up into the heavens.

Then He explained that He wasn't speaking of a *physical* eating of His flesh—"the words that I speak to you are spirit, and they are life." When we are "born of the Spirit," we partake of His Body. We *spiritually* "taste and see that the LORD is good" (Psalm 34:8).

Our testimony in this case continues:

Now about the middle of the feast Jesus went up into the temple and taught. And the Jews marveled, saying, "How does this Man know letters, having never studied?" Jesus answered them and said, "My doctrine is not Mine, but His who sent Me. If anyone wants to do His will, he shall know concerning the doctrine, whether it is from God or whether I speak on My own authority."

Then some of them from Jerusalem said, "Is this not He whom they seek to kill?...But look! He speaks boldly, and they say nothing to Him. Do the rulers know indeed that this is truly the Christ? However, we know where this Man is from; but when the Christ comes, no one knows where He is from." Then Jesus cried out, as He taught in the temple, saying, "You both know Me, and you know where I am from; and I have not come of Myself, but He who sent Me is true, whom you do not know. But I know Him, for I am from Him, and He sent Me." Therefore they sought to take Him; but no one laid a hand on Him, because His hour had not yet come. And many of the people believed in Him, and said, "When the Christ comes, will He do more signs than these which this Man has done?" The Pharisees heard the crowd murmuring these things concerning Him, and the Pharisees and the chief priests sent officers to take Him.

On the last day, that great day of the feast, Jesus stood and cried out, saying, "If anyone thirsts, let him come to Me and drink. He who believes in Me, as the Scripture has said, out of his heart will flow rivers of living water." But this He spoke concerning the Spirit, whom those believing in Him would receive; for the Holy Spirit was not yet given, because Jesus was not yet glorified.

Then the officers came to the chief priests and Pharisees, who said to them, "Why have you not brought Him?" The officers answered, "No man ever spoke like this Man!" (John 7:14–17,25–32,37–39,45,46)

Again, Jesus is affirming His incarnation. A normal man would say something like, "For this purpose I was born..." But Jesus claimed that He *came* from God. After this the Jewish leaders sent officers to arrest Him, but after hearing Jesus speak they came back empty-handed, saying, "No man ever spoke like this Man!" How true.

> Jesus answered them, "Most assuredly, I say to you, whoever commits sin is a slave of sin. A slave does not abide in the house forever, but a son abides forever. Therefore if the Son makes you free, you shall be free indeed. I know that you are Abraham's descendants, but you seek to kill Me, because My word has no place in you. I speak what I have seen with My Father, and you do what you have seen with your father."
>
> They answered and said to Him, "Abraham is our father." Jesus said to them, "If you were Abraham's children, you would do the works of Abraham. But now you seek to kill Me, a Man who has told you the truth which I heard from God. Abraham did not do this. You do the deeds of your father." Then they said to Him, "We were not born of fornication; we have one Father—God."
>
> Jesus said to them, "If God were your Father, you would love Me, for I proceeded forth and came from God; nor have I come of Myself, but He sent Me. Why do you not understand My speech? Because you are not able to listen to My word. You are of your father the devil, and the desires of your father you want to do. He was a murderer from the beginning, and does not stand in the truth, because there is no truth in him. When he speaks a lie, he speaks from his own resources, for he is a liar and the father of it." (John 8:34–44)

These were the religious leaders, the epitome of piety. They were the religious elite, and He was telling them that God wasn't their Father. They instead were children of the devil. No wonder they wanted to kill Him.

> "But because I tell the truth, you do not believe Me. Which of you convicts Me of sin? And if I tell the truth, why

do you not believe Me? He who is of God hears God's words; therefore you do not hear, because you are not of God." Then the Jews answered and said to Him, "Do we not say rightly that You are a Samaritan and have a demon?"

Jesus answered, "I do not have a demon; but I honor My Father, and you dishonor Me. And I do not seek My own glory; there is One who seeks and judges. Most assuredly, I say to you, if anyone keeps My word he shall never see death." (John 8:45–51)

Again, we now are forced to leave off any thought that this man is a great teacher. These are not the words of a great teacher or a great man. He said that "anyone" who does what He says would never die.

As this discourse between Jesus of Nazareth and the religious leaders begins to draw to a close, I must explain something. It is an understatement to say that the Jews highly esteemed God's name. They wouldn't even say it because it was so holy. Even today, some Orthodox Jews won't *speak* or even write the name of G-d.

When Moses discovered the burning bush on the holy mountain, he heard the words, "Moses, Moses!...Take your sandals off your feet, for the place where you stand is holy ground." It was the voice of God, the voice of the Holy One who made all things... and He was speaking to one man. This was the God who made the lightning, created every atom, and spoke the massive sun and every star into being. This is the Creator of the infinite universe, the one who is omnipresent throughout His creation. This is the God who made the human eye, with its 137,000,000 light-sensitive cells, the Creator of the amazing human brain, with its unbelievable sophistication. He is the One who sees every thought of every human being, knows how many hairs are upon every head, every intention of every heart, and promises to bring every work into judgment, including every secret thing.

God told Moses that He wanted him to deliver Israel out of the hand of the Egyptians. Moses wasn't excited about this. Besides not being a good spokesperson, he was very concerned Israel wouldn't believe that the God of the Universe had actually spoken to him, so he asked, "Who shall I say sent me?" Then Almighty God gave him His name.

He said, "I AM WHO I AM. Thus you shall say…, 'I AM has sent me to you'" (Exodus 3:14). The name of our Creator is "I AM." In other words, God is not "I WAS," or "I WILL BE." He is not bound by mere time. He doesn't have to wait for the future as we do, or look back to the past. He dwells in eternity. Time is a dimension that He created, and He isn't subject to it. It beckons at *His* command. There is no one like Him, and no words can describe His power, His glory, or His incredible holiness.

With these thoughts in mind, listen to the following words from the lowly Carpenter from Nazareth:

> Then the Jews said to Him, … "Are You greater than our father Abraham, who is dead? And the prophets are dead. Whom do You make Yourself out to be?" Jesus answered, "If I honor Myself, My honor is nothing. It is My Father who honors Me, of whom you say that He is your God. Yet you have not known Him, but I know Him. And if I say, 'I do not know Him,' I shall be a liar like you; but I do know Him and keep His word. Your father Abraham rejoiced to see My day, and he saw it and was glad."
>
> Then the Jews said to Him, "You are not yet fifty years old, and have You seen Abraham?" Jesus said to them, "Most assuredly, I say to you, before Abraham was, I AM." Then they took up stones to throw at Him; but Jesus hid Himself and went out. (John 8:52–59)

Do you see what He said? He maintained that the esteemed father of the Hebrew race rejoiced to see His day. Abraham looked forward in time to when the Messiah would be born, and he expressed great joy—he rejoiced at the thought of Jesus of Nazareth. That was enough to enrage the religious leaders, but He hadn't yet reached the climax.

Jesus then said, "Before Abraham was, I AM." What? What did He say? Did He just claim the name that Almighty God gave to Moses for Himself? Jesus, the Carpenter from Nazareth, claimed to be Almighty God, humanity's Creator in human form! He had the audacity—the epitome of unspeakable impudence—to take upon Himself the name of "I AM." That's why the Jews took up stones to throw at Him.

> And many of them said, "He has a demon and is mad. Why do you listen to Him?"...Jesus answered them, "...My sheep hear My voice, and I know them, and they follow Me. And I give them eternal life, and they shall never perish; neither shall anyone snatch them out of My hand. My Father, who has given them to Me, is greater than all; and no one is able to snatch them out of My Father's hand. I and My Father are one." (John 10:20,27–30)

The Bible tells us that there was a division among them. Jesus was either guilty of blasphemy or He was who He said He was. There was no middle ground. He then said that He and God are one, and the Jews predictably picked up stones again to stone Him to death for blasphemy.

In the next bit of testimony that the apostle John records, Lazarus had been dead for four days. Listen to what Jesus said, just as He was about to raise Lazarus from the dead:

> Jesus said to [Martha], "Your brother will rise again." Martha said to Him, "I know that he will rise again in the resurrection at the last day." Jesus said to her, "I am the resurrection and the life. He who believes in Me, though he may die, he shall live. And whoever lives and believes in Me shall never die. Do you believe this?" (John 11:23–26)

Jesus wasn't simply saying that He will raise all the dead, but that He was the actual "Resurrection" itself, the source of all life. Any living person who believes in Him would never die. He then continues:

> But Jesus answered them, saying, "The hour has come that the Son of Man should be glorified. Most assuredly, I say to you, unless a grain of wheat falls into the ground and dies, it remains alone; but if it dies, it produces much grain. He who loves his life will lose it, and he who hates his life in this world will keep it for eternal life. If anyone serves Me, let him follow Me; and where I am, there My servant will be also. If anyone serves Me, him My Father will honor. Now My soul is troubled, and what shall I say? 'Father, save Me from this hour'? But for this purpose I came to this hour... And I, if I am lifted up from the earth, will draw all peoples to Myself." This He said, signifying by what death He would die. (John 12:23–27,32,33)

Here He speaks of His own death, His fears, and even the form that His death will take. He will be "lifted up" (crucified), and will then draw *all* men to Himself. Stay with me as I begin to draw my case to a close:

> Nevertheless even among the rulers many believed in Him, but because of the Pharisees they did not confess Him, lest they should be put out of the synagogue; for they loved the praise of men more than the praise of God. Then Jesus cried out and said, "He who believes in Me, believes not in Me but in Him who sent Me. And he who sees Me sees Him who sent Me. I have come as a light into the world, that whoever believes in Me should not abide in darkness. And if anyone hears My words and does not believe, I do not judge him; for I did not come to judge the world but to save the world.

"He who rejects Me, and does not receive My words, has that which judges him; the word that I have spoken will judge him in the last day. For I have not spoken on My own authority; but the Father who sent Me gave Me a command, what I should say and what I should speak. And I know that His command is everlasting life. Therefore, whatever I speak, just as the Father has told Me, so I speak." (John 12:42–50)

The Bible here pinpoints one major reason men are ashamed to say they belong to Jesus Christ. This is very applicable to the scarcity of believers in Jesus Christ in Hollywood: "For they loved the praise of men more than the praise of God." Here comes Jesus' exclusivity:

Thomas said to Him, "Lord, we do not know where You are going, and how can we know the way?" Jesus said to him, "I am the way, the truth, and the life. No one comes to the Father except through Me. If you had known Me, you would have known My Father also; and from now on you know Him and have seen Him."

Philip said to Him, "Lord, show us the Father, and it is sufficient for us." Jesus said to him, "Have I been with you so long, and yet you have not known Me, Philip? He who has seen Me has seen the Father; so how can you say, 'Show us the Father'?" (John 14:5–9)

In one sentence, Jesus just swept away all the great religions. No one can get to God without Him. He is the only mediator between God and men.[313] Then He again affirms His deity by saying that if they had seen Him they had seen God. Jesus continues:

"And I will pray the Father, and He will give you another Helper, that He may abide with you forever; the Spirit of truth, whom the world cannot receive, because it neither sees Him nor knows Him; but you know Him, for He dwells with you and will be in you. I will not leave you orphans; I will come to you. A little while longer and the world will see Me no more, but you will see Me. Because I live, you will live also. At that day you will know that I am in My Father, and you in Me, and I in you. He who has My commandments and keeps them, it is he who loves Me. And he who loves Me will be loved by My Father, and I will love him and manifest Myself to him."

Judas (not Iscariot) said to Him, "Lord, how is it that You will manifest Yourself to us, and not to the world?" Jesus answered and said to him, "If anyone loves Me, he will keep My word; and My Father will love him, and We will come to him and make Our home with him. He who does not love Me does not keep My words; and the word which you hear is not Mine but the Father's who sent Me." (John 14:16–24)

Here's the ultimate challenge when it comes to the issue at hand. Jesus said, "He who has My commandments and keeps them, it is he who loves Me. And he who loves Me will be loved by My Father, and I will love him and manifest Myself to him." Do what He says—repent and trust in Him—and He will supernaturally reveal Himself to you through the power of the Holy Spirit. Again, that's either true or it isn't.

"If the world hates you, you know that it hated Me before it hated you. If you were of the world, the world would love its own. Yet because you are not of the world, but I chose you out of the world, therefore the world hates you. Remember the word that I said to you, 'A servant is not greater than his master.' If they persecuted Me, they will also persecute you. If they kept My word, they will keep yours also. But all these things they will do to you for My name's sake, because they do not know Him who sent Me ... These things I have spoken to you, that you should not be made to stumble. They will put you out of the synagogues; yes, the time is coming that whoever kills you will think that he offers God service." (John 15:18–21; 16:1,2)

Here is another clue why Christians are not prevalent in Hollywood. The world hates Jesus Christ and those who belong to Him. For evidence, just watch any movie and see how many times you hear the name of Mohammad or Buddha used as a cuss word. Look for a despising of the name of Hitler or the Dalai Lama. Then listen to the name "Jesus Christ" used incessantly in place of a four-letter filth word to express disgust.

Jesus then predicts that His followers would be put to death because they belong to Him. History affirms the truth of this, from Nero feeding Christians to lions and using them as human torches, to the Spanish Inquisition, where multitudes of true believers were tortured to death by the Roman Catholic church.

> Jesus spoke these words, lifted up His eyes to heaven, and said: "Father, the hour has come. Glorify Your Son, that Your Son also may glorify You, as You have given Him authority over all flesh, that He should give eternal life to as many as You have given Him. And this is eternal life, that they may know You, the only true God, and Jesus Christ whom You have sent. I have glorified You on the earth. I have finished the work which You have given Me to do. And now, O Father, glorify Me together with Yourself, with the glory which I had with You before the world was." (John 17:1–5)

Again, He says that He was given power over all humanity, that the definition of eternal life is to know Him and the Father, and that He pre-existed eternally with God before He was born. The following exchange occurred during Jesus' trial:

> Then Pilate said to Him, "Are You not speaking to me? Do You not know that I have power to crucify You, and power to release You?" Jesus answered, "You could have no power at all against Me unless it had been given you from

above. Therefore the one who delivered Me to you has the greater sin." (John 19:10,11)

The Lamb of God, who had stood silently before Pontius Pilate, broke the silence by informing the Roman governor that he had power over Him only because God had given it to him. I'm sure you're familiar with the outcome of that trial. Jesus, though Pilate could find no fault in Him, was put to an agonizing death on the cross. Yet our case doesn't end there.

> And after eight days His disciples were again inside, and Thomas with them. Jesus came, the doors being shut, and stood in the midst, and said, "Peace to you!" Then He said to Thomas, "Reach your finger here, and look at My hands; and reach your hand here, and put it into My side. Do not be unbelieving, but believing." And Thomas answered and said to Him, "My Lord and my God!" Jesus said to him, "Thomas, because you have seen Me, you have believed. Blessed are those who have not seen and yet have believed." (John 20:26–29)

So there you have it. I rest my case. There is the evidence from just one of the four Gospels. You are the judge: what is your verdict? Bring down the gavel. There is no fence upon which to sit. If Jesus of Nazareth is guilty of the charge of blasphemy, sentence Him to death according to the Law. If He is speaking the truth, proclaim Him innocent...and then fall at His feet and say with Thomas and General Lew Wallace, "My Lord and my God."

CONCLUSION

T he following is a list of celebrities who have gone before us. It is very sobering to read their names, each of which stirs warm memories. Yet they are all dead and gone. Think about that. We still admire them, but their fame means nothing to them now. They are gone forever. They are in eternity. The only thing that matters is, *what did they do with Jesus Christ?*

- Alan Hale, Jr. (actor) — Cancer; died January 2, 1990
- Barbara Stanwyck (actress) — Died January 20, 1990
- Ava Gardner (actress) — Pneumonia; died January 25, 1990
- Sammy Davis, Jr. (actor/singer) — Cancer; died May 16, 1990
- Danny Thomas (actor/producer) — Heart attack; died February 6, 1991
- Michael Landon (actor) — Cancer; died July 1, 1991
- Lee Remick (actress) — Cancer; died July 2, 1991
- Redd Foxx (actor) — Heart attack; died October 11, 1991
- Fred MacMurray (actor) — Pneumonia; died November 5, 1991
- Chuck Connors (actor) — Cancer; died November 10, 1992
- Audrey Hepburn (actress) — Cancer; died January 20, 1993
- Andre the Giant (wrestler/actor) — Died January 27, 1993
- Stewart Granger (actor) — Cancer; died August 16, 1993
- Raymond Burr (actor) — Cancer; died September 12, 1993
- Vincent Price (actor) — Cancer; died October 25, 1993
- Bill Bixby (actor/director) — Cancer; died November 21, 1993
- Cesar Romero (actor) — Died January 1, 1994
- Pat Buttram (actor) — Kidney failure; died January 8, 1994

- Telly Savalas (actor) — Cancer; died January 22, 1994
- John Candy (actor/comedian) — Heart attack; died March 4, 1994
- Jessica Tandy (actress) — Cancer; died September 11, 1994
- Burt Lancaster (actor) — Heart attack; died October 20, 1994
- Ginger Rogers (actress/dancer) — Died April 25, 1995
- Lana Turner (actress) — Cancer; died June 29, 1995
- Eva Gabor (actress) — Respiratory distress and other infections; died July 4, 1995
- Dean Martin (singer/actor) — Acute respiratory failure; died December 25, 1995
- Gene Kelly (dancer/actor/director) — Stroke complications; died February 2, 1996
- Juliet Prowse (actress) — Cancer; died September 14, 1996
- Robert Mitchum (actor) — Emphysema and lung cancer; died July 1, 1997
- Jack Lord (actor) — Heart failure; died January 21, 1998
- Lloyd Bridges (actor) — Died March 10, 1998
- George C. Scott (actor) — Died September 22, 1999
- Walter Matthau (actor) — Cardiac arrest; died July 1, 2000
- Sir Alec Guinness (actor) — Cancer; died August 5, 2000
- Jack Lemmon (actor) — Cancer; died June 27, 2001
- Dudley Moore (actor) — Died March 27, 2002
- Rosemary Clooney (singer/actress) — Cancer; died June 29, 2002
- Gregory Peck (actor) — Died June 12, 2003
- Bob Hope (comedian/actor) — Pneumonia; died July 27, 2003
- Charles Bronson (actor) — Died August 30, 2003
- Hope Lange (actress) — Died December 19, 2003
- Peter Ustinov (actor/writer) — Heart failure; died March 28, 2004
- Tony Randall (actor) — Died May 17, 2004

SAVE YOURSELF SOME PAIN

I t is my sincere hope that you have made peace with God through trusting in Jesus Christ. Becoming a Christian is the most incredible event that will ever take place in your life. If you have obeyed the gospel, by turning from your sins and placing your trust in Jesus Christ, *you have found everlasting life!* Be assured, God will never leave you nor forsake you. He has brought you this far and He will complete the wonderful work He has begun in you. God knows your every thought, your every care, and your deepest concerns.

Let's look at some of those possible concerns. First, and of primary concern to you and I, do you have "assurance" of your salvation? We are told to "make your calling and election *sure*" (2 Peter 1:10, emphasis added), so let's go through a short "checklist" to make sure that you are truly saved in the biblical sense:

- Are you aware that God became flesh in the person of Jesus Christ (1 Timothy 3:16), and that He died for the sins of the world?
- Did you come to the Savior because you had sinned against God?
- Did you "repent" and put your faith (trust) in Jesus?
- Are you convinced that He suffered and died on the cross for your sins, and that He rose again on the third day?

Following are additional important principles that can save you a great deal of pain.

1. FEEDING ON THE WORD—DAILY NUTRITION

A healthy baby has a healthy appetite. If you have truly been "born" of the Spirit of God, you will have a healthy appetite. We are told, "As newborn babes, desire the pure milk of the word, that you may grow thereby" (1 Peter 2:2). Feed yourself daily without fail. Job said, "I have treasured the words of His mouth more than my necessary food" (Job 23:12). The more you eat, the quicker you will grow, and the less bruising you will have. Speed up the process and save yourself some pain—vow to read God's Word every day, without fail. Say to yourself, "No Bible, no breakfast. No read, no feed." Be like Job, and put your Bible *before* your belly. If you do that, God promises that you will be like a fruitful, strong, and healthy tree (see Psalm 1). Each day, find somewhere quiet and thoroughly soak your soul in the Word of God.

There may be times when you read through its pages with great enthusiasm, and other times when it seems dry and even boring. But food profits your body whether you enjoy it or not. As a child, you no doubt ate desserts with great enthusiasm. Perhaps vegetables weren't so exciting. If you were a normal child, you probably had to be encouraged to eat them at first. Then, as you matured in life you learned to discipline yourself to eat vegetables. This is because they physically benefit you, even though they may not bring pleasure to your taste buds.

2. FAITH—ELEVATORS CAN LET YOU DOWN

When a young man once said to me, "I find it hard to believe some of the things in the Bible," I smiled and asked, "What's your name?" When he said, "Paul," I casually answered, "I don't believe you." He looked at me questioningly. I repeated, "What's your name?" Again he said, "Paul," and again I answered, "I don't believe you." Then I asked, "Where do you live?" When he told me, I said, "I don't believe that either." His reaction, understandably, was anger. I said, "You look a little upset. Do you know why? You're upset because I didn't believe what you told me. If you tell me that your name is Paul, and I say, 'I don't believe you,' it means that I think you are a liar. You are trying to deceive me by telling me your name is Paul, when it's not."

Then I told him that if he, a mere man, felt insulted by my lack of faith in his word, how much more does he insult Almighty God by refusing to believe His Word. In doing so, he was saying that God isn't worth trusting—that He is a liar and a deceiver. The Bible says, "He who does not believe God has made Him a liar" (1 John 5:10). It also says, "Beware, brethren, lest there be in any of you an evil heart of unbelief..." (Hebrews 3:12). Martin Luther said, "What greater insult...can there be to God, than not to believe His promises."

I have heard people say, "But I just find it hard to have faith in God," not realizing the implications of their words. These are the same people who often accept the daily weather forecast, believe the newspapers, and trust their lives to a pilot they have never seen whenever they board a plane. We exercise faith every day. We rely on our car's brakes. We trust history books, medical books, and elevators. Yet elevators can let us down. History books can be wrong. Planes can crash. How much more then should we trust the sure and true promises of Almighty God. He will never let us down...if we trust Him.

Cynics often argue, "You can't trust the Bible—it's full of mistakes." It is. The first mistake was when man rejected God, and the Scriptures show men and women making the same tragic mistake again and again. It's also full of what *seem* to be contradictions. For example, the Scriptures tell us that "with God, nothing shall be impossible" (Luke 1:37); there is nothing Almighty God can't do. Yet we are also told that it is "impossible for God to lie" (Hebrews 6:18). So there *is* something God cannot do! Isn't that an obvious "mistake" in the Bible? The answer to this dilemma is found in the lowly worm.

Do you know that it would be impossible for me to eat worms? I once saw a man on TV butter his toast, then pour on a can of live, fat, wriggling, blood-filled worms. He carefully took a knife and fork, cut into his moving meal, and ate it. It made me feel sick. It was disgusting. The thought of chewing cold, live worms is so repulsive, so distasteful, I can candidly say it would be impossible for me to eat them, although I have seen it done. It is so abhorrent, I draw on the strength of the word "impossible" to substantiate my claim.

Lying, deception, bearing false witness, etc., is so repulsive to God, so disgusting to Him, so against His holy character, that the Scriptures draw on the strength of the word "impossible" to substantiate the claim. He cannot, could not, and would not lie. That means in a world where we are continually let down, we can totally rely on, trust in, and count on His promises. They are sure, certain, indisputable, true, trustworthy, reliable, faithful, unfailing, dependable, steadfast, and an anchor for the soul. In other words, you can truly believe them, and because of that, you can throw yourself blindfolded and without reserve into His mighty hands. He will never, *ever* let you down. Do you believe that?

3. EVANGELISM—OUR MOST SOBERING TASK

Late in December 1996, a large family gathered in Los Angeles for a joyous Christmas. There were so many gathered that night, five of the children slept in the converted garage, kept warm during the night by an electric heater placed near the door.

During the early hours of the morning, the heater suddenly burst into flames, blocking the doorway. In seconds the room became a blazing inferno. A frantic 911 call revealed the unspeakable terror as one of the children could be heard screaming, "I'm on fire!" The distraught father rushed into the flames to try to save his beloved children, receiving burns to 50 percent of his body. Tragically, all five children burned to death. They died because steel bars on the windows had thwarted their escape. There was only one door, and it was blocked by the flames.

Imagine you are back in time, just minutes before the heater burst into flames. You peer through the darkness at the peaceful sight of five sleeping youngsters, knowing that at any moment the room will erupt into an inferno and burn the flesh of horrified children. Can you in good conscience walk away? No! You *must* awaken them, and warn them to run from that death trap! If you don't warn them, you are breaking the law.

The world sleeps peacefully in the darkness of ignorance. There is only one Door by which they may escape death. The steel bars of sin prevent their salvation, and at the same time call for the flames of eternal justice. What a fearful thing Judgment Day will be! The fires of the wrath of Almighty God will burn for eternity. The Church has been entrusted with the task of awakening them before it's too late. We cannot turn our backs and walk away in complacency. Think of how the father ran into the flames. His love knew no bounds. Our devotion to the sober task God has given us will be in direct proportion to our love for the lost. There are only a few who run headlong into the flames to warn them to flee (Luke 10:2). *Please* be one of them. We really have no choice. The apostle Paul said, "Woe is me if I do not preach the gospel!" (1 Corinthians 9:16).

If you and I ignore a drowning child and let him die when we had the ability to save him, we are guilty of the crime of "depraved indifference." God forbid that any Christian should be guilty of that crime when it comes to those around us who are perishing. We have an obligation to reach out to them. The "Prince of Preachers," Charles Spurgeon, said, "Have you no wish for others to be saved? Then you are not saved yourself. Be sure of that." A Christian *cannot* be apathetic about the salvation of the world. The love of God in him will motivate him to seek and save that which is lost.

You probably have a limited amount of time after your conversion to impact your unsaved friends and family with the gospel. After the initial shock of your conversion, they will put you in a neat little ribbon-tied box, and keep you at arm's length. So it's important that you take advantage of the short time you have while you still have their ears.

Here's some advice that may save you a great deal of grief. As a new Christian, I did almost irreparable damage by acting like a wild bull in a crystal showroom. I bullied my mom, my dad, and many of my friends into making a "decision for Christ." I was sincere, zealous, loving, kind, and stupid. I didn't understand that salvation doesn't come through making a "decision," but through repentance, and that repentance is God-given (2 Timothy 2:25). The Bible teaches that no one can come to the Son unless the Father "draws" him (John 6:44). If you are able to get a "decision" but the person has no conviction of sin, you will almost certainly end up with a stillborn on your hands. In my "zeal without knowledge" I actually inoculated the very ones I was so desperately trying to reach.

There is nothing more important to you than the salvation of your loved ones, and you don't want to blow it. If you do, you may find that you don't have a second chance. Fervently pray for them, asking God for their salvation. Let them see your faith. Let them feel your kindness, your genuine love, and your gentleness. Buy gifts for no reason. Do chores when you are not asked to. Go the extra mile. Put yourself in their position. You know that you have found everlasting life—*death has lost its sting!* Your joy is unspeakable. But as far as they are concerned, you've been brainwashed and have become part of a weird sect. So your loving actions will speak more loudly than ten thousand eloquent sermons.

For this reason you should avoid *verbal* confrontation until you have knowledge that will guide your zeal. Pray for wisdom and for sensitivity to God's timing. You may have only one shot, so make it count. Keep your cool. If you don't, you may end up with a lifetime of regret. *Believe* me. It is better to hear a loved one or a close friend say, "Tell me about your faith in Jesus Christ," rather than you saying, "Sit down. I want to talk to you." Continue to persevere in prayer for them, that God would open their eyes to the truth.

Remember also that you have the sobering responsibility of speaking to other people's loved ones. Perhaps another Christian has prayed earnestly that God would use a faithful witness to speak to his beloved mom or dad, and *you* are that answer to prayer. You are the true and faithful witness God wants to use.

We should share our faith with others *whenever* we can. The Bible says that there are only two times we should do this: "in season and out of season" (2 Timothy 4:2). The apostle Paul pleaded for prayer for his own personal witness. He said, "[Pray] for me, that utterance may be given to me, that I may open my mouth boldly to make known the mystery of the gospel, for which I am an ambassador in chains; that in it I may speak boldly, as I ought to speak" (Ephesians 6:19,20).

Never lose sight of the world and all its pains. Keep the fate of the ungodly before your eyes. Too many of us settle down on a padded pew and become introverted. Our world becomes a monastery without walls. Our friends are confined solely to those within the Church, when Jesus was the "friend of sinners." So take the time to deliberately befriend the lost for the sake of their salvation. Remember that each and every person who dies in his sins has an appointment with the Judge of the Universe. Hell opens wide its terrible jaws. There is no more sobering task than to be entrusted with the gospel of salvation—working with God for the eternal well-being of dying humanity.

The Key

Many Christians have thought, *There must be a key to reaching the lost.* There is—and it's rusty through lack of use. The Bible does actually call it "the key," and its purpose is to bring us to Christ, to unlock the Door of the Savior (see John 10:9). Much of the Church still doesn't even know it exists. Not only is it biblical, but it can be shown through history that the Church used it to unlock the doors of revival. The problem is that it was lost around the turn of the twentieth century. Keys have a way of getting lost. Jesus used it. So did Paul (Romans 3:19,20) and James (James 2:10). Stephen used it when he preached (Acts 7:53). Peter found that it had been used to open the door to release 3,000 imprisoned souls on the Day of Pentecost. Jesus said that the lawyers had "taken away" the key, and had even refused to use it to let people enter into the Kingdom of God (Luke 11:52). The Pharisees didn't take it away; instead, they bent it out of shape so that it wouldn't do its work (Mark 7:8). Jesus returned it to its true shape, just as the Scriptures prophesied that He would do (Isaiah 42:21). Satan has tried to prejudice the modern Church against the key. He has maligned it, misused it, twisted it, and, of course, hidden it—he hates it because of what it does. Perhaps you are wondering what this key is. I will tell you. All I ask is that you set aside your traditions and prejudices and look at what God's Word says on the subject.

In Acts 28:23 the Bible tells us that Paul sought to persuade his hearers "concerning Jesus, both out of the law of Moses, and out of the prophets." Here we have two effective means of persuading the unsaved "concerning Jesus."

Let's first look at how the prophets can help persuade sinners concerning Jesus. Fulfilled prophecy *proves* the inspiration of Scripture. The predictions of the prophets present a powerful case for the inspiration of the Bible. Any skeptic who reads the prophetic words of Isaiah, Ezekiel, Joel, etc., or the words of Jesus in Matthew 24 cannot but be challenged that this is no ordinary book.

The other means by which Paul persuaded sinners concerning Jesus was "out of the law of Moses." We are told that the Law of Moses is good if it is used lawfully (1 Timothy 1:8). It was given by God as a "tutor" to bring us to Christ (Galatians 3:24). Paul wrote that he "would not have known sin except through the law" (Romans 7:7). The Law of God (the Ten Commandments) is evidently the "key of knowledge" Jesus spoke of in Luke 11:52. He was speaking to "lawyers"—those who should have been teaching God's Law so that sinners would receive the "knowledge of sin," and thus recognize their need for the Savior.

Prophecy speaks to the *intellect* of the sinner, while the Law speaks to his *conscience*. One produces *faith* in the Word of God; the other brings *knowledge* of sin in the heart of the sinner. The Law is the God-given "key" to unlock the Door of salvation. You may have noticed that I used this principle in this book.

4. PRAYER—"WAIT FOR A MINUTE"

As I mentioned earlier in this book, God always answers prayer. Sometimes He says yes; sometimes He says no; and sometimes He says, "Wait for a minute." And since God is outside the dimension of time, a thousand years is the same as a day to Him (see 2 Peter 3:8)—which could mean a ten-year wait for us. So ask in faith, but rest in peace-filled patience.

Surveys show that more than 90 percent of Americans pray daily. No doubt they pray for health, wealth, happiness, etc. They also pray when Grandma gets sick, so when Grandma doesn't get better (or dies), many end up disillusioned or bitter. This is because they don't understand what the Bible says about prayer. It teaches, among other things, that our sin will keep God from even hearing our prayers (Psalm 66:18), and that if we pray with doubt, we will not get an answer (James 1:6,7). Here's how to be heard:

- Pray with faith (Hebrews 11:6).

- Pray with clean hands and a pure heart (Psalm 24:3,4).

- Pray genuine heartfelt prayers, rather than vain repetitions (Matthew 6:7).

- Make sure you are praying to the God revealed in the Scriptures (Exodus 20:3–6).

How do you "pray with faith"? If someone says to you, "You have great faith in God," they may think they are paying you a compliment. But they aren't—the compliment is to God. For example, if I said, "I'm a man of great faith in my doctor," it's actually the doctor I'm complimenting. If I have great faith in him, it means that I see him as being a man of integrity, a man of great ability; he is trustworthy. I give "glory" to the man through my faith in him. The Bible says that Abraham "did not waver at the promise of God through unbelief, but was strengthened in faith, giving glory to God, and being fully convinced that what He had promised He was also able to perform" (Romans 4:20,21). Abraham was a man of great faith in God. Remember, that is not a compliment to Abraham. He merely caught a glimpse of God's incredible ability, His impeccable integrity, and His wonderful faithfulness to keep every promise He makes. Abraham's faith gave "glory" to a faithful God.

As far as God is concerned, if you belong to Jesus, you are a VIP. You can boldly come before the throne of grace (Hebrews 4:16). You have access to the King because *you are the son or daughter of the King.* When you were a child, did you have to grovel to get your needs met by your mom or dad? I hope not.

So, when you pray, don't say, "Oh, God, I *hope* you will supply my needs." Instead say something like, "Father, thank You that You keep every promise You make. Your Word says that you will supply *all* my needs according to Your riches in glory by Christ Jesus [Philippians 4:19]. Therefore, I thank You that You will do this thing for my family. I ask this in the wonderful name of Jesus. Amen."

The great missionary Hudson Taylor said, "The prayer power has never been tried to its full capacity. If we want to see Divine power wrought in the place of weakness, failure, and disappointment, let us answer God's standing challenge, 'Call unto me, and I will answer you, and show you great and mighty things of which you know not of.'"

How do you get "clean hands and a pure heart"? Simply by confessing your sins to God, through Jesus Christ, whose blood cleanses us from all our sin (1 John 1:7–9). When you confess them to God through Jesus, God will not only forgive your every sin, He promises to *forget* them (Hebrews 8:12). He will count it as though you had never sinned in the first place. He will make you pure in His sight—sinless. He will even "purge" your conscience, so that you will no longer have that sense of guilt that you sinned. That's why you need to soak yourself in Holy Scripture; read the letters to the churches and see the wonderful things God has done for us through the cross of Calvary. If you don't bother to read the "will," you won't have any idea what has been given to you.

How do you pray "genuine heartfelt prayers"? Simply by keeping yourself in the love of God. If the love of God is in you, you will never pray hypocritical or selfish prayers. In fact, you won't have to pray selfish prayers if you have a heart of love, because when your prayer-life is pleasing to God, He will reward you openly (Matthew 6:6). Just talk to your heavenly Father as candidly and intimately as a young child, nestled on Daddy's lap, would talk to his earthly father. How would you feel if every day your child pulled out a pre-written statement to dryly recite to you, rather than pouring out the events and emotions of that day? God wants to hear from your heart.

How do you know you're praying to "the God revealed in Scripture"? Study the Bible. Don't accept the image of God portrayed by the world, even though it appeals to the natural mind. A loving, kind fatherly-figure, with no sense of justice or truth, appeals to guilty sinners. Look to the thunderings and lightnings of Mount Sinai. Gaze at Jesus on the cross of Calvary—hanging in unspeakable agony because of the justice of a holy God. Such thoughts tend to banish idolatry.

5. WARFARE—PRAISE THE LORD AND PASS THE AMMUNITION

When you became a Christian, you stepped right into the heat of an age-old battle. You now have a threefold enemy: the world, the flesh, and the devil. Let's look at these three resistant enemies.

Our first enemy is the world. When the Bible speaks of the "world" in this context, it is referring to the sinful, rebellious, world system. This is the world that loves the darkness and hates the light (John 3:20), and is governed by the "prince of the power of the air" (Ephesians 2:2). The Bible says that the Christian has escaped the corruption that is in the world through lust. "Lust" is unlawful desire, and is the life's blood of the world—whether it be the lust for sexual sin, for power, for money, for material things. Lust is a monster that will never be gratified, so don't feed it. It will grow bigger and bigger until it weighs heavy upon your back, and will be the death of you (James 1:15).

There is nothing wrong with sex, power, money, or material things, but when desire for these becomes predominant, it becomes idolatry (Colossians 3:5). We are told, "Do not love the world or the things in the world. If anyone loves the world, the love of the Father is not in him," and, "Whoever therefore wants to be a friend of the world makes himself an enemy of God" (1 John 2:15; James 4:4).

The second enemy is the devil. As we have seen, he is known as the "god of this age" (2 Corinthians 4:4). He was your spiritual father before you joined the family of God (John 8:44, Ephesians 2:2). Jesus called the devil a thief who came to steal, kill, and destroy (John 10:10).

The way to overcome him and his demons is to make sure you are outfitted with the spiritual armor of God listed in Ephesians 6:10–20. Become intimately familiar with it. Sleep in it. Never take it off. Bind the sword to your hand so you never lose its grip. The reason for this brings us to the third enemy.

The third enemy is what the Bible calls the "flesh." This is your sinful nature. The domain for the battle is your mind.

If you have a mind to, you *will* be attracted to the world and all its sin. The mind is the control panel for the eyes and the ears, the center of your appetites. All sin begins in the "heart" (Proverbs 4:23; Matthew 15:19). We think of sin before we commit it. The Bible warns that lust brings forth sin, and sin when it's conceived brings forth death. Every day of life, we have a choice. To sin or not to sin —that is the question. The answer to the question of sin is to have the fear of God. If you don't fear God, you will sin to your sinful heart's delight.

Did you know that God kills people? He killed a man for what he did sexually (Genesis 38:9,10), killed another man for being greedy (Luke 12:15–21), and killed a husband and wife for telling one lie (Acts 5:1–10). Knowledge of God's goodness—His righteous judgments against evil—should put the fear of God in us and help us not to indulge in sin.

If we know that the eye of the Lord is in every place beholding the evil and the good, and that He will bring every work to judgment, we will live accordingly. Such weighty thoughts are valuable, for "by the fear of the LORD one departs from evil" (Proverbs 16:6). Jesus said,

> "And I say to you, My friends, do not be afraid of those who kill the body, and after that have no more that they can do. But I will show you whom you should fear: Fear Him who, after He has killed, has power to cast into hell; yes, I say to you, fear Him!" (Luke 12:4,5)

6. Fellowship—Flutter by Butterfly

Pray about where you should fellowship. Make sure the place you select as your church home calls sin what it is—sin. Do they believe the promises of God? Are they loving? Does the pastor treat his wife with respect? Is he a man of the Word? Does he have a humble heart and a gentle spirit? Listen closely to his teaching. It should glorify God, magnify Jesus, and edify the believer.

One evidence that you have been truly saved is that you will have a love for other Christians (1 John 3:14). You will want to fellowship with them. The old saying that "birds of a feather flock together" is true of Christians. You gather together for the breaking of bread (communion), for teaching from the Word, and for fellowship. You share the same inspirations, illuminations, inclinations, temptations, aspirations, motivations, and perspirations—you are working together for the same thing: the furtherance of the Kingdom of God on earth. This is why you attend church—not because you have to, but because you want to.

Don't become a "spiritual butterfly." Send your roots down. If you are flitting from church to church, how will your pastor know what type of food you are digesting? We are told that your shepherd is accountable to God for you (Hebrews 13:17), so make yourself known to your pastor. Pray for him regularly. Pray also for his wife, his family, and the church leaders. Being a pastor is no easy task. Most people don't realize how many hours it takes to prepare a fresh sermon each week. They don't appreciate the time spent in prayer and in the study of the Word. If the pastor makes the same joke twice, or shares something he has shared before, remember, he's human. So give him a great deal of grace, and double honor. Never murmur about him. If you don't like something he has said, pray about it, then leave the issue with God. If that doesn't satisfy you, leave the church, rather than divide it through murmuring and complaining.

A woman once spread some hot gossip about a local pastor. What he had supposedly done became common knowledge around town. Then she found that what she had heard wasn't true. She gallantly went to the pastor and asked for his forgiveness. The pastor forgave her, but then told her to take a pillow full of tiny feathers to a corner of the town, and in high winds, shake the feathers out. Then he told her to try to pick up every feather. He explained that the damage had already been done. She had destroyed his good reputation, and trying to repair the damage was like trying to pick up feathers in high winds.

The Bible says that there is life and death in the power of the tongue (Proverbs 18:21). We can kill or make something alive with our words. The Scriptures also reveal that God hates those who cause division among believers (Proverbs 6:16). Pray with the psalmist, "Set a guard, O LORD, over my mouth; keep watch over the door of my lips" (Psalm 141:3).

Remember the old saying, "He who gossips to you will gossip about you."

7. THANKSGIVING—DO THE RIGHT THING

For the Christian, every day should be Thanksgiving Day. We should be thankful even in the midst of problems. The apostle Paul said, "I am exceedingly joyful in all our tribulation" (2 Corinthians 7:4). He knew that God was working all things together for his good, even though he was going through trials (Romans 8:28).

Problems *will* come your way. God will see to it personally that you grow as a Christian. He will allow storms in your life, in order to send your roots deep into the soil of His Word. We also pray more in the midst of problems. It's been well said that you will see more from your knees than on your tiptoes.

A man once watched a butterfly struggling to get out of its cocoon. In an effort to help it, he took a razor blade and carefully slit the edge of the cocoon. The butterfly escaped from its problem —and immediately died. It is God's way to have the butterfly struggle. It is the struggle that causes its tiny heart to beat fast and to send the life's blood into its wings.

Trials have their purpose. They make us struggle—they bring us to our knees. They are the cocoon in which we often find ourselves. It is there that the life's blood of faith in God helps us spread our wings.

Faith and thanksgiving are close friends. If you have faith in God, you will be thankful because you know His loving hand is upon you, even though you are in a lion's den. That will give you a deep sense of joy, and joy is the barometer of the depth of faith you have in God. Let me give you an example. Imagine if I said I'd give you one million dollars if you sent me an email. Of course, you don't believe I would do that, but imagine if you did. Imagine if you knew 1,000 people who had sent me an email, and every one received their million dollars—no strings attached. More than that, you actually called me, and I assured you personally that I would keep my word. If you believed me, wouldn't you have joy? If you didn't believe me—no joy. The amount of joy you have would be a barometer of how much you believed my promise.

We have so much for which to be thankful. God has given us "exceedingly great and precious promises" that are "more to be desired than gold." Do yourself a big favor: believe those promises, thank God continually for them, and "let your joy be full."

8. WATER BAPTISM—SPRINKLE OR IMMERSE?

The Bible says, "Repent, and let every one of you be baptized in the name of Jesus Christ for the remission of sins..." (Acts 2:38). There is no question about whether you should be baptized. The questions are how, when, and by whom?

It would seem clear from Scripture that those who were baptized were fully immersed in water. Here's one reason why: "Now John also was baptizing in Aenon near Salim, because there was much water there" (John 3:23). If John were merely sprinkling believers, he would have needed only a cupful of water. Baptism by immersion pictures our death to sin, burial, and resurrection to new life in Christ (see Romans 6:4, Colossians 2:12). The Philippian jailer and his family were baptized at midnight, the same hour they believed. The Ethiopian eunuch was baptized as soon as he believed (Acts 8:35–37), as was Paul (Acts 9:17,18). Baptism is a step of obedience, and God blesses our obedience. So what are you waiting for?

Who should baptize you? It is clear from Scripture that other believers had the privilege, but check with your pastor, he may want the honor himself.

9. Tithing—The Final Frontier

It has been said that the wallet is the "final frontier." It is the final area to be conquered—the last thing that we surrender to God. Jesus spoke much about money. He said that we cannot serve God and mammon (Matthew 6:24). The word "mammon" was the common Aramaic word for riches, which is related to a Hebrew word signifying "that which is to be trusted." In other words, we cannot trust God and money. Either money is our source of life, our great love, our joy, our sense of security, the supplier of our needs—or God is.

When you open your purse or wallet, give generously and regularly to your local church. A guide to how much you should give can be found in the "tithe" of the Old Testament: 10 percent of your income. Whatever amount you give, make sure you give *something* to the work of God (see Malachi 3:8–10). Give because you want to, not because you have to. God loves a cheerful giver (2 Corinthians 9:7), so learn to hold your money with a loose hand.

10. Troubleshooting—Cults, Atheists, Skeptics

If you know the Lord, nothing will shake your faith. It is true that the man with an experience is not at the mercy of a man with an argument. If you are converted, and the Holy Spirit "bears witness" that you are a child of God (Romans 8:16), you will never be shaken by a skeptic.

When cults tell you that you must acknowledge God's name to be saved, that you must worship on a certain day, or that you must be baptized by an elder of their church, don't panic. Merely go back to the Instruction Manual. The Bible has all the answers, and searching them out will make you grow.

If you feel intimidated by atheists—if you think they are "intellectuals"—read my book *God Doesn't Believe in Atheists*. It will reveal that they are the opposite. It will also show you how to prove God's existence, and also prove that the "atheist" doesn't exist.

Finally, the way to prevent sporting injury and pain is to keep yourself fit. Exercise. The apostle Paul kept fit through exercise. He said, "Herein do I exercise myself, to always have a conscience void of offense toward God, and toward men" (Acts 24:16, KJV). Do the same. Listen to the voice of your conscience. It's your friend, not your enemy. Remember these words of Solomon: "Fear God and keep His commandments, for this is the whole duty of man. For God will bring every work into judgment, including every secret thing, whether it is good or whether it is evil" (Ecclesiastes 12:13,14).

Keep the Day of Judgment before your eyes. On that Day, you will be glad that you cultivated a tender conscience.

I hope these principles have been helpful and that they will some day save you some pain.

For a complete list of books, tapes, DVDs, and other products by Ray Comfort, visit www.livingwaters.com, call 800-437-1893, or write to: Living Waters Publications, P.O. Box 1172, Bellflower, CA 90706.

Also be sure to visit www.whatHollywoodbelieves.com for more exciting information.

PSALM 51

Perhaps you have made it this far, and you still haven't made peace with God. This could be because you are not sure what to pray. You may want to make Psalm 51 you personal prayer of repentance. This is King David's apology to God after he sinned by committing adultery with Bathsheba and having her husband murdered.

Have mercy upon me, O God, according to Your loving-kindness; according to the multitude of Your tender mercies, blot out my transgressions. Wash me thoroughly from my iniquity, and cleanse me from my sin.

For I acknowledge my transgressions, and my sin is always before me. Against You, You only, have I sinned, and done this evil in Your sight; that You may be found just when You speak, and blameless when You judge.

Behold, I was brought forth in iniquity, and in sin my mother conceived me. Behold, You desire truth in the inward parts, and in the hidden part You will make me to know wisdom.

Purge me with hyssop, and I shall be clean; wash me, and I shall be whiter than snow. Make me hear joy and gladness, that the bones You have broken may rejoice. Hide Your face from my sins, and blot out all my iniquities.

Create in me a clean heart, O God, and renew a steadfast spirit within me. Do not cast me away from Your presence, and do not take Your Holy Spirit from me.

Restore to me the joy of Your salvation, and uphold me by Your generous Spirit. Then I will teach transgressors Your ways, and sinners shall be converted to You.

Deliver me from the guilt of bloodshed, O God, the God of my salvation, and my tongue shall sing aloud of Your righteousness. O Lord, open my lips, and my mouth shall show forth Your praise. For You do not desire sacrifice, or else I would give it; You do not delight in burnt offering.

The sacrifices of God are a broken spirit, a broken and a contrite heart; these, O God, You will not despise. Do good in Your good pleasure to Zion; build the walls of Jerusalem. Then You shall be pleased with the sacrifices of righteousness, with burnt offering and whole burnt offering; then they shall offer bulls on Your altar.

NOTES

1. "AP Poll: Most prefer phrase 'under God,'" The Associated Press, March 24, 2004 <www.boston.com/news/nation/washington/articles/2004/03/24/ ap_poll_most_prefer_phrase_under_god>.

2. David W. Moore, The Gallup Organization, March 12, 2004 <www.gallup.com/content/login.aspx?ci=10963>.

3. Sharon Waxman, "Hollywood Rethinking Faith Films After 'Passion,' *New York Times*, March 15, 2004, Section E, p. 1.

4. Cecil B. DeMille, "American Epic: Biography Documentary Special," April 5, 2004.

5. *Newsweek*, July 1992, as quoted on <www.geocities.com/RegnevaT/pp/ television.htm>.

6. The Center for Media and Public Affairs, "The Elite and How to Avoid It," *Newsweek*, July 20.

7. If you find additional data, please feel free to send it to me at findout@whatHollywoodbelieves.com.

8. Quoted by Alfred Armand Montepert, *Distilled Wisdom* (Englewood Cliffs, NJ: Prentice Hall Inc., 1965), p. 36.

9. Quoted by Gary DeMar, *America's Christian History: The Untold Story* (Atlanta, GA: American Vision Publishers, Inc., 1993), p. 60.

10. Quoted by Robert Flood, *The Rebirth of America* (Philadelphia: Arthur S. DeMoss Foundation, 1986), p. 37. Tryon Edwards, D.D., *The New Dictionary of Thoughts: A Cyclopedia of Quotations* (Garden City, NY: Hanover House, 1852), p. 48.

11. Letter to Thomas Jefferson, December 25, 1813.

12. Tryon Edwards, *The New Dictionary of Thoughts*, p. 47.

13. Interview by Bill Moyers, "Of Myth and Men," *Time* magazine, April 26, 1999, as quoted on <www.next-wave.org/may99/starwars.htm>.

14. Ibid.

15. Interview by Rick Clark, "The Gospel According to Dolly Parton," August 1, 2002 <www.mixonline.com/ar/audio_gospel_according_dolly/>.

16. NBC-TV's *Today* Show, March 1995, as quoted on
    <www.scientology.org/scnnews/scn_new.htm#TRAVOLTA>.

17. Interview by Mark Lawson, "Celebrities and Their Faith"
    <www.bbc.co.uk/religion/interviews/travolta.shtml>.

18. Ibid.

19. Ibid.

20. Interview by The Cranky Critic <www.crankycritic.com/qa/arnold.html>.

21. Ibid.

22. Interview by Rebecca Phillips, "A Spiritual Recovery"
    <www.beliefnet.com/story/135/story_13540_2.html>.

23. Ibid.

24. Interview by Bill Flanagan, *Rolling Stone,* July 10–24, 1997, p. 51
    <www.james-taylor.com/text/rs7-97.txt>.

25. Ibid.

26. Interview by Ron Rosenbaum, *Playboy* magazine, March 1978, as quoted on
    <www.interferenza.net/bcs/interw/play78.htm>.

27. Interview by Bruce Heiman, KMEX Radio, December 7, 1979
    <www.interferenza.net/bcs/interw/79-dec7.htm>.

28. Interview by *Playboy* magazine, 1969, as quoted on
    <www.positiveatheism.org/hist/quotes/quote-s6.htm>.

29. Interview by Camille Paglia in the *Advocate,* as quoted on
    <www.celebatheists.com/entries/atheist_35.html>.

30. Interview by Anthony DeCurtis, February 20, 2001
    <www.beliefnet.com/story/67/story_6758_4.html>.

31. Ibid.

32. Interview by Joseph B. Mauceri <www.horrorking.com/interview1.html>.

33. Interview by Paul Fischer <www.girl.com.au/bruce_almighty.htm>.

34. Ibid.

35. Ibid.

36. See Romans 2:15.

37. Interview by Chris Colin, *Salon,* December 28, 1998.

38. "The 12-Minute Playboy Philosophy," *Playboy,* January 2004, quoted on
    <www.ronaldbrucemeyer.com/rants/1210almanac.htm>.

39. *Playboy* magazine, January 2000, as quoted on
    <www.celebatheists.com/entries/ambiguous_4.html>.

40. Ephesians 5:22,25.

41. See Ephesians 5:28,29.

42. Proverbs 5:18–20.

43. Interview by Phil Boatwright "Holy Hollywood!" <www.saworship.com/article-page.php?ID=1026&Page=search.php>.

44. Word Records <www.wordrecords.com/billyraycyrus>.

45. Probably a reference to the Fourth of the Ten Commandments.

46. Michael Jackson, "My Childhood, My Sabbath, My Freedom," December 6, 2000 <www.beliefnet.com/story/56/story_5697_2.html>.

47. Ibid <www.beliefnet.com/story/56/story_5697_3.html>.

48. Romans 1:20.

49. Hebrews 11:6.

50. Interview by *Vanity Fair*, 1992, as quoted on <www.celebatheists.com/entries/atheist_26.html#5>.

51. Ephesians 2:1; 4:18.

52. See Romans 8:16.

53. See 1 John 5:12,13.

54. Halle Berry Quotations <www.absolutely.net/berry/quote.htm>.

55. Charlton Heston Presents the Bible <www.hestonbible.com/homepage.asp>.

56. Hebrews 2:14,15, NIV.

57. Revelation 1:18.

58. Interview by ivillage.com, "Maria Shriver: Talking to Kids About Death," June 21, 2001 <www.ivillage.com/books/intervu/celeb/articles/0,,200922_19346,00.html?arrivalSA=1&cobrandRef=0&arrival_freqCap=1&pba=adid=7052080>.

59. Maria Shriver, *What's Heaven?* (Golden Books, 1999).

60. Interview by Anne A. Simpkinson, "Trying to Capture the Invisible," as quoted on <www.beliefnet.com/story/95/story_9558_4.html>.

61. Acts 19:24–28.

62. Interview by Jill Bartlett, "Getting to Know Lisa Whelchel," Crosswalk.com <www.lisawhelchel.com/lkinterview2.html>.

63. Ibid.

64. Ibid.

65. Craig Miller, "An Interview with Shaun Cassidy: American Gothic, Roar, and More!" *Spectrum*, Vol. 1, #13, May 1998, as quoted on <www.members.aol.com/Eccentric3/spectrum13.html>.

66. Interview by Blase DiStefano, *OutSmart* magazine, August 1998, as quoted on <http://home.houston.rr.com/blase/Root%20Folder/debbie.html>.

67. "Mel Gibson's Great Passion," March 6, 2003, as quoted on <www.zenit.org/english/visualizza.phtml?sid=32330>.

68. Interview by Graham Fuller, "The Not-So-Rough Cut," January 2000, as quoted on <www.findarticles.com/cf_dls/m1285/1_30/58929062/p2/ article.jhtml?term=>.

69. Ibid.

70. Ibid.

71. Romans 3:23; 5:12.

72. John 8:34; 2 Peter 2:19.

73. Romans 8:2.

74. Dan Ewald, *Today's Christian,* November/December 2002, as quoted on <www.christianitytoday.com/tc/2002/006/3.38.html>.

75. Ibid.

76. Interview by Alberlynne "Abby" Harris, October 2003 <www.blackfilm.com/20031031/features/laurence_keanu.shtml>.

77. Wooding, "Screen legend Jane Russell hopes the success of *The Passion of the Christ* will 'wake up' Hollywood producers," March 26, 2004 <www.assistnews.net/Stories/s04030103.htm>.

78. Marc Morano, "Hollywood Actress Declares Herself 'Right Wing Christian Bigot,'" Cybercast News Service, February 03, 2003 <www.cnsnews.com/ViewCulture.asp?Page=\Culture\archive\200302\CUL20030203c.html>.

79. Interview by Steven Waldman, Beliefnet, June 15, 2000 <www.belief.net/story/29/story_2919_1.html>.

80. Ibid.

81. Isaiah 7:14; Matthew 1:23; Luke 1:26–35.

82. See John 3:13; 6:38; 6:51; 1 Corinthians 15:47.

83. Interview by *Wichita Times,* April 3, 1995, as quoted on <www.scientology.org/scnnews/scn_new.htm#KIRSTIE>.

84. Interview by Steven Waldman, Beliefnet, September 12, 2003 <www.beliefnet.com/story/132/story_13244_3.html>.

85. Ibid.

86. Ibid.

87. As quoted on <www.tinseltownonline.com/web_tv/clip.asp?id=60>.

88. Christina Dalton, "When the Roll Is Called Down Yonder," *Los Angeles Times,* January 11, 2004, as quoted on <www.almenconi.com/news/jan04/011804.html>.

89. Colossians 1:21.

90. Interview by Robert H. Schuller, "Hour of Power," September 16, 1984 <www.hourofpower.org/interviews/gregory_peck.html>.

91. Ibid.

92. Ibid.

93. Interview by Wilson Morales, "Gods and Generals: An Interview with Robert Duvall," February 2003 <www.blackfilm.com/20030221/features/robertduvall.shtml>.

94. Online interview on Yahoo, March 19, 1998 <www.peoplejustlikeus.org/Tv_and_Movies/Robert_Duvall.html>.

95. Ibid.

96. See John 5:24; Romans 6:13; Ephesians 2:4,5; Colossians 2:13.

97. Interview by John Meroney and Patricia Beauchamp <www.taemag.com/issues/articleid.17708/article_detail.asp>.

98. Ibid.

99. Loretta Young Quotations <www.absolutely.net/Loretta_Young/quote.htm>.

100. Interview by Stewart Weiner, "Tribute to Loretta Young," *Palm Springs Life*, December 1995 <www.palmspringslife.com/whisper/loretta.html>.

101. John 19:30.

102. Acts 20:21.

103. "Los Angeles Salutes Jimmy Stewart," *Scouting* magazine, October 1980, p. 55, as quoted on <www.members.aol.com/t915/Inspire/Stewart.htm>.

104. As quoted on <http://miguel_coias.tripod.com/BradPitt.html>.

105. Interview by Chris Heath, "The Unbearable Bradness of Being," *Rolling Stone*, October 28, 1999, p. 66, as quoted on <http://pittcenter.com/magazines/rs99/index.htm>.

106. As quoted on <www.biblebabble.curbjaw.com/miscquotes.htm>.

107. Charles Chaplin, *My Autobiography* (New York: Simon & Schuster, 1964), p. 291.

108. Steve Turner, "The Ballad of John and Jesus," *Christianity Today*, June 12, 2000 <www.christianitytoday.com/ct/2000/007/34.86.html>.

109. Geoffrey Giuliano, *Lennon in America* (Lanham, MD: Cooper Square Press, 2000), p. 134.

110. Steve Turner, "The Ballad of John and Jesus."

111. Interview by *Playboy* magazine, as quoted on <www.johnlennon.it/playboy_interview.htm>.

112. See James 4:15.

113. U.S. Census Bureau, World Vital Events <www.census.gov/cgi-bin/ipc/pcwe>.

114. Walt Disney, "Deeds Rather Than Words," <www.startedbyamouse.com/archives/WaltPrayer.shtml>.

115. Walt Disney, "Prayer in My Life" <www.startedbyamouse.com/archives/WaltPrayerOriginal.shtml>.

116. Walt Disney, "Deeds Rather Than Words" <www.startedbyamouse.com/archives/WaltPrayer.shtml>.

117. Interview by Dennis Hughes, *Share Guide* <www.shareguide.com/MacLaine.html>.

118. Shirley MacLaine, "Spirit: The Other Side of Life" <www.shirleymaclaine.com/spirituality/spirit.html>.

119. Shirley MacLaine, "Reincarnation Survey" <www.shirleymaclaine.com/reincarnation/reincarnsurvey.html>.

120. Interview with Liz Sterling <www.innerviewsonline.com/maclaine.html>.

121. Ephesians 2:2.

122. See John 3:1–5; Galatians 3:26.

123. John 1:12,13.

124. Interview by E! Online <www.eonline.com/Celebs/Qa/JanetJackson/interview2.html>.

125. Interview by Larry King, "Larry King Live," October 19, 2002 <www.cnn.com/TRANSCRIPTS/0210/19/lklw.00.html>.

126. Edna Gundersen, "Madonna's Epiphany," *USA Today*, April 17, 3003 <www.usatoday.com/life/2003-04-17-madonna-main_x.htm>.

127. Romans 13:14.

128. 1 John 3:4.

129. Gundersen, "Madonna's Epiphany," *USA Today*.

130. Meg Grant, "A Time to Heal," *Reader's Digest*, May 2004, p. 81.

131. Romans 8:28.

132. John Wayne Quotes <http://millennium.fortunecity.com/savannah/731/jwayne/quotes.html>.

133. Interview by Barbara Walters, 1979, as quoted on <www.members.aol.com/fortscott/quotes.htm>.

134. Interview by Bonnie Churchill, *The Christian Science Monitor*, May 5, 2000 <www.csmonitor.com/durable/2000/05/05/p19s2.htm>.

135. Anne Marie Cruz, "Passion's Play," *People* magazine, May 3, 2004, p. 148.

136. Dick Cavett and Christopher Porterfield, *Cavett* (New York: Bantam Books, 1974), p. 56.

137. Ephesians 2:8,9.

138. John 6:28,29.

139. Interview in Las Vegas, 1999, as quoted on <www.shotokankata.com/Articles/Chuck%20Norris%20Interview.htm>.

140. "The Battle Over Citizen Kane" documentary, 1996, written and produced by Thomas Lennon, Richard Ben Cramer, and Michael Epstein.

141. As quoted on <www.brainyquote.com/quotes/authors/o/orson_welles.html>.

142. See 2 Timothy 1:9, Titus 1:2.

143. Interview by Larry King, as quoted on <www.wilder.narod.ru/index_interview_larry.htm>.

144. Interview by the *New England Skeptics Society* newsletter, Summer 1998, as quoted on <www.celebatheists.com/entries/atheist_36.html>.

145. Interview by *Movieline*, May 1994 <www.alec.helenheart.com/movieline94_en.html>.

146. Ibid.

147. Interview by *Ladies' Home Journal,* October 1991, p. 215 <www.ronaldbrucemeyer.com/rants/0512almanac.htm>.

148. Genesis 1:1.

149. Psalm 14:1.

150. Paul Lee Tan, *Encyclopedia of 7700 Illustrations*, as quoted on <www.tanbible.com/tol_ill/tol_ill_godexistenceof.htm>.

151. Interview by *Playboy* magazine, August 1993, as quoted on <www.geocities.com/Hollywood/Lot/2976/pb1993.html>.

152. Marlon Brando, *Brando: Songs My Mother Taught Me* (New York: Random House, 1994), p. 76.

153. Ibid., p. 97,98.

154. Stephen Hawking, *A Brief History of Time* (Bantam Doubleday Dell, 1988).

155. Carl Boberg, "How Great Thou Art," © 1953, Manna Music Inc.

156. Proverbs 9:10.

157. Psalm 128:1–4.

158. Interview by Larry King, "Larry King Live," April 25, 2004 <www.cnn.com/TRANSCRIPTS/0404/25/lkl.00.html>.

159. Tasha Robinson, "Is There a God?" *The Onion A.V. Club*, October 9, 2002 <www.theonionavclub.com/feature/index.php?issue=3837&f=1>.

160. John 17:3.

161. *Billboard Magazine*, December 4, 1994, as quoted on <www.celebatheists.com/entries/ambiguous_5.html>.

162. Interview by Larry King, "Larry King Live," March 9, 2003 <www.cnn.com/TRANSCRIPTS/0303/09/lklw.00.html>.

163. "Absolution" is a doctrine of the Roman Catholic church.

164. Interview by Joe Hyams, *Playboy*, February 1962, as quoted on <www.sinatraarchive.com/tis/play-interview.html>.

165. William Hall, *Raising Caine: An Authorized Biography (*Englewood Cliffs, NJ: Prentice-Hall, Inc., 1981), quoted on <www.quinnell.us/religion/famous/cd.html>.

166. *Washington Post,* May 17, 1998, as quoted on Pete Aiken's Hollywood Report <www.postfun.com/pfp/lcb/0698.html>.

167. Personal interview, May 1, 2004.

168. Interview by *George* magazine, July 1998 <www.celebatheists.com/entries/ambiguous_9.html>.

169. Ibid.

170. 2 Corinthians 5:17.

171. Philippians 2:13.

172. Ray Comfort, *The Evidence Bible* (Gainesville, FL: Bridge-Logos Publishers, 2001), pp. 585–586.

173. Grant R. Jeffery, *The Signature of God.*

174. Combined from Matthew 24; Mark 13; Luke 21; 1 Timothy 4; and 2 Timothy 3.

175. See 2 Peter 2:1–3.

176. See 2 Peter 3:1–7.

177. Interview by Randy Hill and John Peyton, *Connection* magazine, January 2002 <www.connectionmagazine.org/2002_01/ts_kathy_ireland.htm>.

178. Ibid.

179. Sharon Waxman, "George Clooney, Uncowled," *The Washington Post,* September 28, 1997.

180. Ibid.

181. See John 8:31,32.

182. Interview by Stephen Sato, "Della Reese Spreads Her Wings" <www.thebostonchannel.com/sh/entertainment/ontheset/ entertainment-ontheset-20001002-113329.html>.

183. Ibid.

184. David Kristof and Todd Nickerson, *Predictions for the Next Millennium: Thoughts on the 1,000 Years Ahead from Today's Celebrities* (Kansas City, MO: Andrews McMeel Publishing, 1998).

185. Interview by Larry King, "Larry King Live," August 18, 2002 <www.cnn.com/TRANSCRIPTS/0208/18/lklw.00.html>.

186. Interview by Larry King, "Larry King Live," January 2, 2003 <www.cnn.com/TRANSCRIPTS/0301/02/lkl.00.html>.

187. Ibid.

188. Interview by Larry King, "Larry King Live," February 5, 2002 <www.cnn.com/TRANSCRIPTS/0202/05/lkl.00.html>.

189. Ibid.

190. Stephen Thompson, "Is There a God?" *The Onion A.V. Club,* October 9, 2002 <www.theonionavclub.com/feature/index.php?issue=3837&f=1>

191. As quoted on <www.geocities.com/Heartland/Farm/5645/willieaames.html>.

192. Ibid.

193. Neil Simon, *Rewrites: A Memoir* (Simon & Schuster, 1996).

194. Interview by Larry King, "Larry King Live," August 30, 2002 <www.cnn.com/TRANSCRIPTS/0208/30/lkl.00.html>.

195. Exodus 20:7.

196. See my book *God Doesn't Believe in Atheists: Proof That the Atheist Doesn't Exist* (Bridge-Logos Publishers). Contact us if you know Carrie Fisher, and we would be more than happy to send her a complementary copy.

197. John Winokur (ed.), *The Portable Curmudgeon Redux* (New York: E. P. Dutton, 1992).

198. For a greater understanding of this, freely listen to "Hell's Best Kept Secret" online at www.livingwaters.com.

199. Paul Rifkin, *The God Letters* (Warner Books, 1986).

200. Interview by Larry King, "Larry King Live," July 30, 2002 <www.cnn.com/TRANSCRIPTS/0207/30/lkl.00.html>.

201. Ibid.

202. Interview by *Rolling Stone* magazine, 1987, as quoted on <www.atheism.about.com/library/quotes/bl_q_WAllen.htm>.

203. Woody Allen, *Without Feathers* (Random House, 1976), as quoted on <www.atheism.about.com/library/quotes/bl_q_WAllen.htm>.

204. For an understanding of why people fall away from the faith, see *The Way of the Master* by Kirk Cameron and Ray Comfort (Tyndale House Publishers).

205. Larry Flynt, *An Unseemly Man* (New York: Newstar Press, 1977).

206. John 16:2,3.

207. Interview by Ramona Cramer Tucker, "Jackie's Gold Medal Faith," *Today's Christian Woman*, September/October 1998, p. 46.

208. Ibid.

209. Ibid.

210. Interview by Larry King, "Larry King Live," May 4, 2002 <www.cnn.com/TRANSCRIPTS/0205/04/lklw.00.html>.

211. Interview by Larry King, "Larry King Live," January 15, 2001 <www.cnn.com/TRANSCRIPTS/0101/15/lkl.00.html>.

212. Interview by Larry King, "Larry King Live," October 6, 2002 <www.cnn.com/TRANSCRIPTS/0210/06/lklw.00.html>.

213. Barnes and Noble/America Online chat with Christopher Reeve, May 7, 1998.

214. Interview by Dan McLeod, *The Georgia Straight*, July 10–17, 1997, p. 43.

215. Interview by *The Memphis Commercial Appeal*, October 23, 1995, as quoted on <www.scientology.org/scnnews/scn_new.htm>.

216. Interview by *Canada's Pride* magazine, quoted on <www.scientology.org/scnnews/scn_new.htm>.

217. Interview by Gary Susman, December 12, 1996 <http://rai.ucuenca.edu.ec/concelt/webpaginas/whitneyint.html>.

218. Ibid.

219. Interview by Anthony DeCurtis <www.beliefnet.com/story/78/story_7870_1.html>.

220. Galatians 5:19–21.

221. See Ephesians 2:8,9.

222. There are some who can't reconcile the fact that a Jewish person can also be a Christian. But when a Chinese person becomes a Christian, he is still Chinese. When a Jewish person becomes a Christian, the blood doesn't drain from his or her veins.

223. As quoted on <www.peoplejustlikeus.org/Tv_and_Movies/Urich.html>.

224. Interview by Larry King, "Larry King Live," October 1996, <www.cnn.com/TRANSCRIPTS/0204/21/lklw.00.html>.

225. Interview by www.celebsite.com, as quoted on <www.peoplejustlikeus.org/Tv_and_Movies/Washington.html>.

226. Ibid.

227. LaTonya Taylor, "The Church of O," *Christianity Today*, April 1, 2002, Vol. 46, No. 4, p. 38.

228. Romans 10:3,4.

229. John 14:6.

230. MSN Entertainment <http://entertainment.msn.com/netcal/?netcal=664>.

231. Interview by Patrick Carr, "The Spirit is Willing," *The Journal of Country Music*, April 14, 2000 <www.stevenmenke.com/TributeCash%20 No%206.htm>.

232. Interview by Paul O'Donnell, June 4, 2003 <www.beliefnet.com/story/127/story_12768_2.html>.

233. Ibid.

234. Ibid.

235. Ibid.

236. C. S. Lewis, *The Case for Christianity* (New York: Macmillan Company, 1944).

237. Interview by David Frost on PBS, November 1995 <www.celebatheists.com/entries/atheist_13.html>.

238. Interview by Lisa Ryan, "The 700 Club," April 27, 2001 <www.angelfire.com/zine/baptistsurfer/Mr.T.html>.

239. Hollywood Jesus, Review of *Babe: Pig in the City*, 1998 <www.hollywoodjesus.com/babe_city.htm>.

240. Laura Deni, "Mickey Rooney: Growing Up Not Growing Old," Broadway to Vegas, May 21, 2000 <www.broadwaytovegas.com/May21,2000.html>.

241. As quoted by Cal Thomas, "The Greatest Story Ever Filmed," August 5, 2003 <www.townhall.com/columnists/calthomas/ct20030805.shtml>.

242. Interview by Larry King, "Larry King Live," November 28, 2003 <www.cnn.com/TRANSCRIPTS/0311/28/lkl.00.html>.

243. Valerie Lawson, "Tom foolery or new faith: James won't say," November 26, 2002 <www.smh.com.au/articles/2002/11/25/1038173697940.html>.

244. Interview by Janet Chismar, "Jim Caviezel Speaks to Broadcasters about Playing Jesus" <www.crosswalk.com/faith/1247507.html>.

245. Ibid.

246. Ibid.

247. Mary Beth Brown, "Reagan's Life Was Saved for a Reason," April 2, 2004 <www.worldnetdaily.com/news/article.asp?ARTICLE_ID=37862>.

248. Interview by Kristi Watts, "Natalie Cole: There Was Something Missing," 2001 <www.cbn.com/700club/features/Natalie_Cole_2001.asp>.

249. Interview by Cheryl Wilcox and Scott Ross, "Barbara Mandrell: Sweetness Through Suffering," August 16, 2002 <www.cbn.com/700club/features/Barbara_Mandrell-interview.asp>.

250. Ibid.

251. Interview by Becky Garrison, "Victoria's Secret (She's a Christian in Hollywood!)," *The Door Magazine*, Sept./Oct. 1999 <www.thedoormagazine.com/archives/victoriajackson.html>.

252. Ibid.

253. Stephen Thompson, "Is There a God?" *The Onion A.V. Club*, October 9, 2002 <www.theonionavclub.com/feature/index.php?issue=3837&f=1>.

254. 1 Corinthians 1:18.

255. See Galatians 3:24.

256. 1 Corinthians 1:26–29.

257. Mark 10:15.

258. Ray Comfort, *The Evidence Bible* (Gainesville, FL: Bridge-Logos Publishers, 2001), p. 101.

259. Interview by Nancy Collins, "In Gere," *Reader's Digest*, February 2003, p. 89,90.

260. Interview by Rajiv Mehrotra, as quoted on Life Positive, April 1996 <www.lifepositive.com/Spirit/world-religions/buddhism/gere.asp>.

261. Ibid.

262. See 2 Thessalonians 1:8–10.

263. Stephen Thompson, "Is There a God?" *The Onion A.V. Club,* October 9, 2002, Vol. 38, Iss. 37 <www.theonionavclub.com/feature/index.php? issue=3837&f=1>

264. Interview with Dan D. Ewald <www.peoplejustlikeus.org/Tv_and_Movies/ Patricia_Heaton.html>.

265. Ibid.

266. Interview by David Kupfer, The Progressive, July 2003 <www.progressive.org/july03/intv0703.html>.

267. Interview by Charles Laurence <www.peoplejustlikeus.org/ Tv_and_Movies/Martin_Sheen.html>.

268. Matthew 25:41.

269. 2 Thessalonians 1:7–9.

270. Hebrews 13:8.

271. Interview by Dan Wooding, ASSIST Ministries, March 22, 2002 <www.assistnews.net/Stories/s02030090.htm>.

272. Interview by Phil Donahue, February 24, 2002 <www.simmins.org/ donahue.html>

273. Ibid.

274. Ibid.

275. Interview by Holly McClure <www.crosswalk.com/fun/1124986.html>.

276. Ibid.

277. "Gere, Goldie Hawn visit Dalai Lama," Metro FM <www.metrofm.co.za/wuzup/celebrity_news/167647.htm>.

278. Ibid.

279. "Alice Cooper Goes With God," *Charisma* News Service, March 1, 2002 <www.worldnetdaily.com/news/article.asp?ARTICLE_ID=26647>.

280. Ibid.

281. Ibid.

282. Interview by Barbara Walters, "20/20," December 4, 1998, as quoted on <www.geocities.com/TelevisionCity/Stage/6196/2020.html>.

283. Ibid.

284. Ibid.

285. Anika Van Wyk, "Fox Faces Battle With Illness," November 26, 1998 <www.canoe.ca/JamMoviesArtistsF/fox_michaelj.html>.

286. 1 Corinthians 2:9.

287. Interview by *Guideposts* <www.christianactivities.com/testimonies/story.asp?ID=1937>.

288. Ibid.

289. Gail Hollenbeck, "Boone Sees God's Hand in Career," *St. Petersburg Times*, March 8, 2003 <www.sptimes.com/2003/03/08/news_pf/Citrus/Boone_sees_God_s_hand.shtml>.

290. Interview by Entertainment Tonight <www.winona.www3.50megs.com/lostsoulint.html>.

291. Ibid.

292. Mark E. Howerter, "The Other Side," 1996 <www.otherside.net/kathylee.htm>.

293. As quoted on <www.peoplejustlikeus.org/Tv_and_Movies/Gifford.html>.

294. Jone Johnson Lewis, "Lily Tomlin Quotations" <www.womenshistory.about.com/library/qu/blqutoml.htm>.

295. Psalm 119:105.

296. Interview by Dan Ewald, "The Rebirth of Kirk Cameron," *Today's Christian* magazine, March/April 2003, Vol. 41, No. 2, p. 20 <www.christianitytoday.com/tc/2003/002/1.20.html>.

297. Ibid.

298. Ibid.

299. Interview by Mim Udovitch, *Rolling Stone* <www.rollingstone.com/features/featuregen.asp?pid=147>.

300. "How Dean Jones Caught the Love Bug," *New Man* magazine, March/April 2000.

301. 2 Corinthians 4:3,4.

302. 2 Timothy 2:26.

303. 1 Corinthians 1:26–29.

304. Luke 10:21.

305. Acts 4:12.

306. John 14:6.

307. Hebrews 11:6.

308. Matthew 5:6.

309. Proverbs 12:28.

310. Revelation 12:10; John 8:44.

311. Philip Schaff, *The Person of Christ: The Miracle of History* (New York: C. Scribner & Co., 1866).

312. Quoted in Josh McDowell, *Evidence That Demands a Verdict* (Nashville, TN: Thomas Nelson, 1999).

313. 1 Timothy 2:5. See also Acts 4:12.